THE
BOG MAN
AND THE
ARCHAEOLOGY OF PEOPLE

THE
BOG MAN
AND THE
ARCHAEOLOGY OF PEOPLE

Don Brothwell

British Museum Publications

© 1986 Don Brothwell

Third impression 1988

Published by British Museum Publications Ltd
46 Bloomsbury Street, London WC1B 3QQ

British Library Cataloguing in Publication Data

Brothwell, D. R.
    The bog man and the archaeology of people.
    1. Lindow Moss (Cheshire) — Antiquities
    2. England — Antiquities
    I. Title   II. British Museum. *Trustees*
    936.2'716   DA690.L6/

        ISBN 0 7141 1384 0

Designed by Adrian Hodgkins

Printed in Great Britain by
Butler & Tanner Ltd, Frome and London

Contents

To the memory of
Maureen Girling, 1950–1985,
friend and collaborator
in the Lindow Man project

Acknowledgements

It is a pleasure to offer my sincere thanks to all those who have assisted in the production of this account of the investigation of Lindow Man and the archaeology of people in general.

Ian Stead of the British Museum kindly invited me to join the Lindow project at an early planning stage, and subsequently read and offered comment on the manuscript of this book. The numerous specialists in the project provided a range of information which I have called on, and I hope used correctly. During the 'formative' stage of gathering and sifting information, I visited or otherwise called on the help of various friends and colleagues, particularly Jim Bourke, Rosalie David, Deirdre O'Sullivan, David Liversage, Andrew Jones, Jack Harbison, Emme Rabino Massa, Tim Holden, Keith Dobney, Malcolm McLeod, Michael Gebühr and Geoffrey Dimbleby. The late 'Sandy' Sandison, master palaeopathologist of mummies, stimulated my interest in this field and provided me with various illustrations, some of which I have used here. Teresa Francis of British Museum Publications has provided that most important of assistance, friendly and proficient editing.

Finally, the wide range of illustrations would not have been possible without the help of colleagues, museums and photographic departments in various parts of the world. These may be listed as follows:

British Museum: 1, 5–7, 12–16, 20, 35, 52, 54, 62, 68–9, 84, I, V; British Museum (Natural History): 18, 47, 66, 92–3, 95; Manchester Museum: 37, 50, 85–6; National Museums of Scotland, Edinburgh: III; Forhistorisk Museum, Moesgård, Denmark: 2, 9–11, 17, 48; National Museum, Copenhagen: 28–30, 71, 78; Silkeborg Museum, Denmark: 8, 22–4, 31; Greenland Museum: 88, VII; Schloss Gottorf, Schleswig, Germany: 4, 21; State Hermitage Museum of Leningrad: 81, IV; Cairo Museum: 56, 94; Provincial Museum of Drenthe, Assen, Netherlands: 77; Hunan Provincial Museum, Changsha, China: 90; Jintan Museum, Jiangsu Province, China: 91; Museum of Anthropology, University of California, Berkeley: 41; Montezuma Castle, Arizona: 97; City University, London (artwork by Meredydd Moores, British Museum): 32–3; by courtesy of Reg Davis, Royal Marsden Hospital: 43–4; Department of Diagnostic Radiology, St Bartholomew's Hospital, London: 46, 57; Department of Diagnostic Radiology, University of Manchester: 45; University of Liverpool: 38–9; Department of Medical Photography, Royal Hospital, Sheffield: 51; Richard Neave/BBC: 36; Heather Angel/Biofotos: II; Deirdre O'Sullivan: 27, 80, VIII, IX; Chief Constable of Cheshire: 3; Dr E. Rabino Massa: 40; Andrew Jones: 58–9; Dr A. W. Pike: 60; Professor G. Dimbleby: 61; Judith Dayton: 63–4; Jim Bourke: 70; Tim Holden: 75–6.

The quotation on page 121 from *The Collected Poems of Stevie Smith* (Penguin Modern Classics) is reproduced by kind permission of the poet's Executor, James MacGibbon.

Introduction

The discovery in Cheshire in 1984 of an ancient bog body and the subsequent detailed television coverage excited the imagination of the public at large. Although it was a single find, without any finery or an elaborate grave, it was distinctive in that it was a body still 'fleshed', rather than the more commonly occurring skeleton. Indeed, there was something a little awe-inspiring about seeing the man gradually emerge in the laboratory from the peat which had covered and protected him for so many centuries. As the final remnants of peat were washed away and the dark skin glistened with moisture, it was easy to visualise the strongly made shoulders and chest filling out and coming to life, entering the twentieth century from a peaty time capsule. It was thus small wonder that a group of scientists of various specialisations accepted the invitation to take part in further 'bringing to life' this man from the bog. The questions they sought to answer were many and varied. When and how did he die? How healthy was he, and what sort of diet did he have? Was anything significant buried with him? While the scientists investigated and sampled and brought in a range of highly sophisticated equipment in an attempt to answer such questions, the British Museum conservation laboratory began the difficult task of ensuring that 'Pete Marsh', as the newspapers had christened him, would not decay and would eventually be presentable for public exhibition.

The following pages convey some of the excitement of the research surrounding this bog man and show the wide range of information gathered so far. While this is a story in itself, it has become clear to me during these investigations that the time has come for some form of stocktaking on archaeological bodies in general. Where have they been found, and what sorts of environment encourage their preservation? What is the state of the art in studying them? Do some tell us more than others, and are some neglected? What are the archaeological prospects for finding more? What special kinds of information can be derived from bodies of this kind which cannot be obtained from all the numerous ancient skeletons? As in other aspects of archaeology, the questions and problems are many.

What follows, then, is an up-to-date account of Lindow Man and his place in worldwide investigations on archaeological bodies. Like all of us, he can be seen as a unique individual or as part of a community, and this book considers him under both of these aspects.

1 The body of Lindow Man, almost fully cleared of peat. Note the decayed left forearm and the positions of the fingernails.

1. A Body is Discovered

There is a story in the Orkney Islands that early in the seventeenth century a young woman from a wealthy family, Mary Linklater, mysteriously disappeared on a moor. Some said she was murdered by her lover, Thomas Irvine, and others that it was the work of two local witches, Kitty Grieve and Mary Richart. All three were known to have been on the moor that night, and the two witches were eventually taken to court but escaped being put to death. However, Kitty Grieve did not live long afterwards, and it is said that before she died she confessed that the illegitimate son of Patrick Stewart, Earl of Orkney, had struck Mary Linklater down while trying to obtain information about family valuables and that the two witches had been compelled to help bury her body in the moor.

W. R. Mackintosh of the island newspaper, the *Orcadian*, took the story up again in May 1864, combining it with another to arrive at a solution to the mystery. For on the fourteenth of that month, one James Craigie had been cutting peats in the vicinity of Mary Linklater's disappearance and had unearthed a pair of roughly made shoes about four feet below the surface. Helpers were called in and they exposed the body of a woman, covered by various items of coarse clothing. The newspaper commented that the woollen clothes and the hair were very well preserved, and when the the body was examined the brain was also found to be in a good state of preservation. But the bones, characteristically of bog bodies, had become 'soft and spongy'. In the eyes of the local press and populace, the murder and the whereabouts of the body were solved. Regrettably, the body has disappeared, no doubt reburied, and one is left wishing that a sample were still available for radiocarbon dating as a final check on the antiquity of this lady.

A remarkably similar story, but with a better archaeological ending, is that of 'Red Christian', a Danish peat-cutter who disappeared in the Grauballe district in 1887. It had been assumed that he had fallen into the bog when drunk, and had drowned as a result of the fatal mixture of water and alcohol! In April 1952, peat-cutters came upon a very well-preserved body near the village of Grauballe and Professor P. V. Glob, famous for his work on bog bodies, and experts from the museum at Aarhus were called in, and the local inhabitants and the press became interested in the find. This combination of archaeologists and local 'folk history' resulted in a good-humoured debate. While Professor Glob and his colleagues identified the find as another ancient bog body, it was linked by others to the disappearance of 'Red Christian', and indeed one elderly lady claimed to recognise him in the features of Grauballe Man. Eventually the carbon 14 laboratory in Copenhagen's National Museum produced dates for Grauballe Man's death of between 1,540 and 1,740 years ago. The debate about Red Christian was over.

The most recent of such confusions was related to a murder involving Lindow Moss in Cheshire, where Lindow Man was later discovered. On 13 May 1983, peat-workers Andy Mould and Stephen Dooley picked a peculiar football-sized lump off an elevator carrying peat to the shredding machine. The old saying 'curiosity killed the cat' took on a bizarre twist in this case, for what they jokingly called a dinosaur's egg turned out after cleaning to be a partly decomposed human head, consisting of an incomplete skull with some hair and with the left eyeball intact.

J. G. Benstead of the Home Office Forensic Science Laboratory

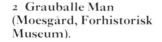

2 Grauballe Man (Moesgård, Forhistorisk Museum).

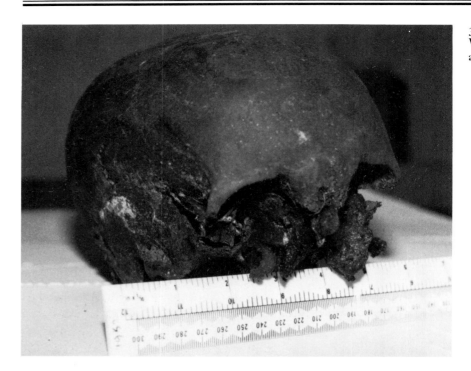

3 The skull of Lindow Woman, before drying-out and shrinkage.

in Southport identified the head as that of a woman, perhaps in the 30–50-year age-group. The discovery was a fateful one for Mr Peter Reyn-Bardt, who had lived close to Lindow Moss with his wife. She had vanished in 1960, and in early 1983 the Macclesfield police were looking further into her disappearance. When told of the discovery of the skull, Mr Reyn-Bardt confessed to her murder. By the end of that year, he had been tried and convicted in Chester Crown Court. The extreme irony of the discovery and subsequent murder confession is that a radiocarbon date for the skull was later obtained by the Oxford University Research Laboratory for Archaeology and the History of Art. It showed that 'Lindow Woman' died around AD 210 ($\pm$ 80 years) and was certainly not Peter Reyn-Bardt's wife.

The Discovery of Lindow Man
At the end of May 1952, at a small peat bog on the Windeby estate in Schleswig, Germany, peat-workers were shovelling machine-cut peat onto their conveyor belt when a workman noticed, but did not recognise, part of a leg. By good fortune the machinery was stopped, and investigation showed that the remains of a foot and a hand had been trimmed off a body buried in the bog. Local authorities and museum specialists were called in, and detailed study began. Once the

police were satisfied that this was not a recent murder victim but an ancient body, they withdrew. Further investigations were thus left to various archaeologists and specialists, co-ordinated by Dr Karl Schlabow.

Over thirty years later, history repeated itself at a peat deposit in Cheshire, for the circumstances of the discovery of Lindow Man were surprisingly similar. Again, thanks to an observant member of staff during processing, the body was saved from being cut to shreds.

Although Lindow Moss once extended over 600 hectares, it is now about a tenth of its former size and mainly covered in birch scrub. It has been common land since medieval times, and its peat has been used as fuel for many centuries. An eighteenth-century writer mentions cases of drowning in the treacherous bog, presumably at the wettest period after winter. Today, the commercial working, employing large Hy-Mac excavators, cuts peat to the depth of about a metre. It is then stacked for six months to dry and mature.

On 1 August 1984, Andy Mould, who a year earlier had found the head of Lindow Woman, picked what looked like a piece of wood off the elevator at the peat-shredding mill. He threw it towards his workmate Eddie Slack, and as it hit the ground, peat fell away to reveal a human foot. The police were called in, and they removed the foot for examination. The county archaeologist, Rick Turner, was also informed and he visited the site without delay. By establishing which peat stack the foot had come from and surveying the nearby

4 The Windeby Girl as she was removed from the site, but still on the supporting block of peat (Schleswig, Schloss Gottorf).

peat section, he was able to locate the rest of the body. Indeed, a flap of skin was still sticking out, although it was rather dark and changed owing to some localised decay after exposure. The body was covered up with wet peat and the police were once more informed. (This new 'corpse' was about 250 metres south-west of the place where the head of Lindow Woman had turned up.) By Monday 6 August, preparations and permissions were all ready, and Lindow Man was excavated out in his peat block within the day. Field archaeologists were assisted by a number of specialists, including the conservationist Velson Horie, palaeobotanists Gill Yates and Nigel Richardson, and human biologist Robert Connolly.

The peat block containing the body was finally cleared and lifted out on a heavy sheet of plywood which had been inserted under it. It took six people to lift it onto the narrow-gauge railway belonging to the industrial site, and it was pulled back to the depot on an open bogey. From there, it was taken to the mortuary of Macclesfield District Council Hospital, where it had to remain until it could be dated.

5 (*above*) The remaining damaged lower leg of Lindow Man.

6 Section of the Lindow peat as left by the peat-cutting machinery. The flap of abdominal skin left exposed can be seen just above the trowel.

7 The site of Lindow Man's discovery, showing the peat block surrounding the body being cut away.

Dating the Find

During the past thirty years, archaeological dating has been revolutionised by the discovery and development of a number of so-called absolute dating methods. Formerly, most techniques for dating objects were of a relative kind, based on stratigraphy, cultural similarities in pottery, coins, or even pollen spectra. Of the newer methods, carbon 14 or radiocarbon dating has had the most tremendous impact, although, as we shall see, it also has its problems.

The radiocarbon method relies on the fact that carbon 14 is constantly being produced from cosmic radiation and then taken up by life forms – either at a primary level during photosynthesis by plants or secondarily during feeding by animals. The method was developed from a theoretical basis by Professor Willard Libby, and it was to earn him a Nobel Prize for chemistry in 1960. He was able to establish that at death, further uptake or exchange of radiocarbon ceases, and the $C14$ then begins to decay at a steady rate. The amount of $C14$ remaining in an object can therefore be measured, providing an ingenious and precise dating method.

15

Table 1	Body	Sex	Date
Some comparative C14 dates for bog bodies	Lindow	M	300 BC
	Grauballe*	M	55 BC
(various sources) *up to ± 100 years should be allowed as a potential error of each estimate*	Huldre Fen	F	95 AD
	Elling	F	205 BC
	Tollund	M	210 BC
	Krogens Molle	F	55 BC
	Haraldskjaermose	F	490 BC
	Borre Fen I	M	840 BC
*without the humic acid extracted, the date was AD 310	Borre Fen II	F	475 BC
	Borre Fen III	F	770 BC

However, although radiocarbon dating is now a well-established technique, it has to be admitted that there may still be difficulties. For instance, in the case of a body, there may not be enough organic material left to provide a date, even though there may be plenty of skeletal material. Moreover, samples can be contaminated in various ways, such as the penetration of bones by unrecognised tree roots or the influence of earlier volcanic activity near sites.

In the case of Lindow Man, plenty of organic material was of course available, both in the body and as peat, and by a strange turn of events no fewer than three laboratories were called upon to undertake radiocarbon dating. Because the C14 laboratory of the British Museum normally works only with large samples (and the analysis is a destructive process), the Oxford University laboratory, which had dated Lindow Woman, was approached in order that their newly developed specialised small-sample C14 accelerator might be used. However, the staff were on vacation, and as the coroner would not release the body from the mortuary in Macclesfield until it had been dated, it was fortunate that Robert Otlet of the Atomic Energy Research Establishment at Harwell was able to take on the work. Accordingly, 6·5 grams of bone from one of the hands and 30 grams of shin bone were delivered to Harwell by the police, and on 17 August it was announced that the body was over 1,000 years old. It was released on 21 August and transported in a wooden box to London, where it had been decided that all further excavation should be carried out at the British Museum.

It was then that the C14 problems developed, for further sampling of the body and associated peat produced a range of dates spanning about 900 years. Dates from the body and from the peat showed some divergence, and one possible explanation was that the peat into which the body sank was some centuries older. However, the peat is likely to have been forming far too quickly for an ancient layer to have come into contact with the body as it gradually submerged. Moreover, there was no evidence that the body had been buried deep into the bog, nor of any peat-cutting which might have allowed it to become associated with a much older layer. The answer is more probably to be found in environmental influences on organic remains and the dating process. New calculations were therefore made, and the body was submitted to further intensive radiocarbon study. It is a reflection of the good relationships between research laboratories of this kind that the Harwell, Oxford and British Museum laboratories all took part in attempting to resolve this question. The discrepancies in the dates for the body have yet to be explained, but there is general agreement that the peat enveloping Lindow Man was formed about 300 BC.

Preservation of the Human Body

The rate of decomposition in a body depends on a variety of factors. For instance, decay may be accelerated when death has resulted from certain types of infection. The presence of flies of the kind that produce maggots can also lead quickly to the loss of flesh. Even in the absence of maggots, a body may putrefy rapidly and the soft tissues 'drip away in their own juices' if the temperature is moderately warm and there is plenty of air. This natural decay can be slowed down by embalming techniques, and even the old method of hardening the tissues in alcohol was effective in this respect. The early Egyptian embalmers used a quite different technique, whereby natural deposits of natron (a carbonate and bicarbonate of sodium, with some impurities) appear to have been applied dry to the body. Such a technique must have enhanced the drying-out process.

Placing the body in an environment without air also slows down decomposition. The anaerobic conditions of bogs can therefore be ideal, depending on the amount of decay occurring before the submergence or burial of a body. Bog water is also generally acid, which may deter some micro-organisms. Very cold water, too, has preserving qualities, and no one with murder in mind should consider disposing of the corpse in the depths of a lake. In warmer surface waters, the body may be nibbled at by fish or other scavengers, and rot will take place more quickly in areas not well covered by clothing. So, in the case of a clothed corpse, hands, feet and head may become skeletonised before the rest of the body.

Temperature can also have other effects. Parts of ancient Scythian bodies have been well preserved in the permafrost conditions of the Altai mountains in Siberia. Similarly, the cold environment of caves high in the Andes has greatly slowed down any changes in the bodies buried there. At the other end of the scale, hot, drying conditions (especially where there is a good air flow) may rapidly desiccate a body. Thus, even predynastic burials in Egypt, 5,000 years old, may be in a remarkably good state of preservation. A body on display at the British Museum and affectionately known to staff as 'Ginger' (Plate V) is a good example of natural warm drying. Other examples have been found in the hot, dry climates of south-west America and Peru. Surprisingly, the warm but more humid environments of the Aleutian Islands and Canary Islands have also encouraged preservation, and indeed one of the best-preserved bodies I have seen was that of an ancient Guanche (Canary Island) mummy.

Occasionally one finds exceptional preservation in unexpected circumstances. A medieval knight found at St Bees Priory in Cumbria was one such case. Although other bodies in the cemetery were reduced to skeletons, the knight had been wrapped in thick shrouds over which a wax and honey preparation had been poured, creating a special micro-environment. The body was then placed in a sealed lead coffin.

No less a person than Oliver Cromwell can be mentioned as an example of preservation in post-medieval bodies in Britain. He died in 1658 and it is recorded that internal decay was rapid and odorous, in spite of embalming. Burial was therefore quickly undertaken, in coffins of lead and wood. This must have greatly slowed down decomposition, for he was in no great state of decay in 1660 when Parliament set into motion an amazing act of revenge. Cromwell and two others were exhumed in 1661 and their 'odious carcasses' trundled to Tyburn and the gallows. After a period of hanging, they were taken down and their heads hacked off. Even allowing for cloth around Cromwell's body, it is nevertheless interesting that it took eight blows to strike off the head, suggesting that much leathery tissue remained on the neck. It is said that the head remained stuck on a pole at Westminster Hall until 1684 and somehow it survived with some flesh and hair on it until 1960, when it was buried at Sidney Sussex College in Cambridge.

Tattooed Maori heads and Torres Strait mummies, of relatively

8 The body of Tollund Man, naked except for a leather cap and belt. Note the decay at the hands and knees, and the rope around his neck (Silkeborg Museum).

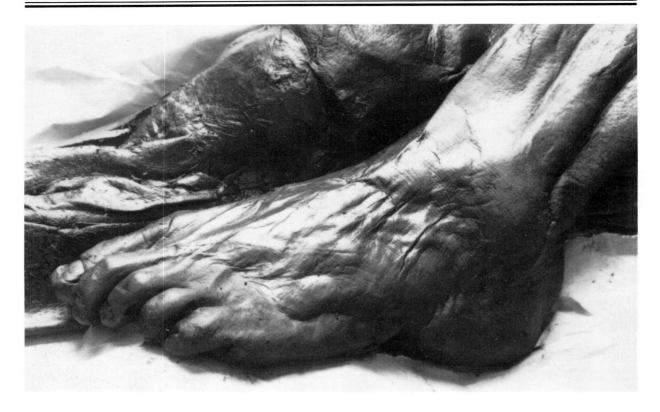

recent date, provide further examples of preserved bodies, and some of the most recent and extraordinary states of preservation have been recorded at the fifteenth-century site of Qilakitsoq in west Greenland, where six women and two children were impeccably preserved by a natural freeze-drying process. Remarkable examples of human preservation also come from China, from Han and Sung dynasty tombs. The Sung tomb of Chou Yü, in Kiangsu province, showed truly remarkable preservation, not only of the body but of numerous silk garments and fabrics, with their colours still bright.

In the case of Lindow Man and the other northern European bog bodies, preservation has been surprisingly good considering the environment, but by no means perfect, and the corpses show varying degrees of decay. Thus, while the Windeby Girl's brain has retained much of its size and shape, and an eye of a man from Borre Fen in Denmark looks blindly from its socket, Lindow Man is less well preserved. Apart from the intestines, the internal organs of bog bodies rarely survive, and even under the skin, the muscles may decompose and become reduced in size. The hands and forearms of Lindow Man have suffered considerable decay, like those of a body found at

9 The little-changed foot of Grauballe Man, showing the relatively short toe-nails.

20

10 The hand of Grauballe Man is relatively long and narrow. It shows evidence of thumb and palm prints and slightly 'rough' nails.

Tollund Fen in Denmark (whose thigh and shin regions were also poorly preserved). In contrast to these, however, the arms and legs of Grauballe Man were in good condition, even if somewhat squashed.

The Microbiology of the Body

To permit detailed examination, the Lindow body had to be removed periodically from the 'cooler', the refrigerated container which normally kept it at a temperature of 4°C. It also had to be exposed during the filming, soon after its arrival in London, of the final stages of its excavation from the peat and the subsequent investigation. Clearly it was crucial to monitor any signs of decay. Dr G. L. Ridgway and his colleagues in the Clinical Microbiology Department of University College Hospital made eleven separate checks on the body over six months to ensure that serious decomposition was not taking place.

Swabs were taken and cultures grown of any micro-organisms present on the body, in the surrounding peat and in the water being used as a dampening agent. Various parts of the body were also checked for localised decay. Fortunately, the micro-organisms identi-

11 Professor Glob preparing the 'tanning' vat for the Grauballe corpse.

fied were soil and water commensals which did not seem to be causing significant damage. These included species of *Pseudomonas*, which were found to be polluting the distilled water being applied to the body, even though it was boiled, chilled and frequently changed! Fungal and yeast organisms identified included species of *Mucor*, *Penicillium*, *Verticillium* and *Candida*. It is surprising how quickly dead and decayed organic remains will attract colonisation by living organisms searching for potential food, and even a species of very small white fly (possibly *Thysanura*) became active on the surface of the body. However, in spite of the presence of these small organisms, the body has suffered no serious changes since it was first removed from the peat.

Preserving the Preserved
After the removal of the body from the acid boggy environment of Lindow Moss which had preserved it for so long, the problem of long-term conservation arose. Attempts to preserve the Danish bog bodies had met with variable success. In the nineteenth century, conservation methods were poor, and the Rendswühren Man found near Kiel in 1871 was simply preserved by smoking and drying. Grauballe Man, on the other hand, found in 1952, was subjected to a 'pit-

tanning' process taking over one and a half years. He was immersed in a bath containing a solution of oak bark. The solution was changed three times, using a total of 1,825 pounds of bark. After what must have been a long, anxious period for museum staff, the oak slime was washed off and he was bathed for a month in a mixture of distilled water and Turkish red oil and impregnated with glycerine, cod liver oil and lanolin. Collodion was injected into some parts of the body to help to retain their shape, and very little shrinkage appears to have occurred. The same cannot, however, be said of the Tollund head, which has suffered an estimated 12% reduction in size.

Very different techniques were used in the conservation of Lindow Man, in particular freeze-drying, which has become an increasingly common procedure in museums and laboratories over the past fifteen years. One of the hands of the Cambridge Guanche mummy was successfully rehydrated and freeze-dried in 1968 by R. H. Harris of the British Museum (Natural History), but the new bog body presented a much greater challenge in the application of this technique. The method is essentially a more sophisticated version of what happens if meat is accidentally left exposed in a domestic freezer. The flesh is at first frozen solid, but the ice gradually vaporises and this results in a gradual drying-out. This natural process can be accelerated in freeze-drying units, and the final result is the complete removal of moisture but without shrinkage of the tissue, internally or externally.

The conservation of the Lindow body was in the hands of Sherif Omar and his colleagues in the Department of Scientific Research and Conservation at the British Museum. After studying the literature on the conservation of organic remains and visiting other scientists in Denmark for discussion, they opted for the following procedure. Experimental samples of pig-skin were immersed in various pre-treatment solutions and then freeze-dried. After drying, the skin samples were checked carefully for shrinkage, and one solution selected for further use. This was 15% polyethylene glycol (PEG) 400 in water, and it was chosen because it did not appear to cause any deposit to form on the skin, nor did it affect the test sample in either flexibility or colour. To prevent distortion, the body was immersed in the solution on a moulded perspex sheet. It was then freeze-dried and finally returned to more normal temperatures, being slowly acclimatised to $19(\pm 2)^{\circ}$ C, with a relative humidity of about 55%. A special display case was designed to monitor and maintain this environment.

2. Clues to a Murder

Although one thinks of police laboratory and Home Office pathology investigations as very different from enquiries on archaeological bodies, in fact they have a lot in common. Both aim to determine when death took place, and what caused it. Both attempt to estimate the age and sex of the individual (no easy matter if the body is decayed or incomplete), and to find out as much as possible about any injuries or disease. Finally, both may seek to build up a picture of the person's original physique.

Forensic scientists can therefore make useful contributions to this aspect of archaeology, and archaeologists, in their turn, can aid modern forensic work by their special knowledge of long-term dating and refined excavation techniques (useful in the case of bodies reduced to broken, buried and scattered skeletal fragments). However, except when dealing with bodies from ancient Egypt or modern times, archaeology is only rarely able to identify an individual precisely. Claims are nevertheless sometimes made that a body is that of a particular known person. For instance, there was a controversy over some bones believed to be those of St Edward the Martyr, king of England AD 975–8. According to legend, Edward's stepmother Elfthryth was responsible for his murder at Corfe Castle in Dorset in 978. He was canonised in 1001. Human remains found at Shaftesbury Abbey in 1932 were claimed to be his, and a study made of them was considered to support the story that he was stabbed in the back and also sustained injuries from being dragged along the ground when his foot got caught in his horse's stirrup. Alas, my own examination of the bones did not help to consolidate these claims. In my opinion, the age at death indicated by the skeletal remains seemed wrong, and the damage to the bones far more likely to have been sustained long after death. Ironically, the bones received international attention recently, not because of differences in skeletal interpretation but because two brothers of the Claridge family contested ownership of the remains in court and members of the exiled Russian Orthodox Church debated whether to adopt these remains as suitably saintly relics (the Church of England and the Catholic Church having turned their backs on the bones)!

Those of us watching in the laboratory as the peat was cleaned away from Lindow Man's body were surprised by the number of external features which suggested that he had met a violent death. After further study and reflection, not all of these features have been interpreted as trauma, although one or two are still a cause for debate. The external evidence has now been complemented by the findings of internal investigations.

The upper abdomen and chest were the first parts of the body to be cleared of peat, and except for the area covered by the arms, the surface of this part of the trunk was relatively intact. A small hole in mid-line, below the ribs, turned out to be the navel, slightly distorted. More important and problematical was a narrow opening about 3 centimetres long in the middle part of the right collar bone (clavicle). Was this a stab wound into the upper chest? It was certainly straight and the sides of the injury looked fairly clean-cut. This side of the body was facing down into the peat, and was thus protected from accidental damage while it lay in the bog. Dr Iain West, the forensic specialist, was not convinced, however, that this gash had been made deliberately, and considered that it could have been caused by *post-mortem* changes in the soft tissue, with localised stress and tearing through to the skin. There certainly was some surface tearing and sagging in part of the soft tissue, indicated by the exposure of bone in the region of the upper nose and eyes. There was also a broken mandible, which may have occurred *post mortem* but cannot be altogether excluded as an injury sustained in life or at death.

Because of its bulbous shape, the head began to appear early in the clearing away of the peat. The hair, which was for the most part fairly short, was plastered down to the scalp. As it was cleared, it became evident that the skin was broken twice in approximately mid-line, a few centimetres from the front margin of the hair. The two close tears could perhaps have been written off as *post-mortem* events, but damage to the bone beneath confirmed that blows from some form of relatively blunt implement had twice split the scalp, broken the bone and driven fragments inwards. These bone pieces could in fact be seen in xeroradiographs and, because of the shrinkage and decay of the brain, were now lodged well down below the wound. Towards the back of the head, there appeared to be some zig-zag splitting under the surface of the skin, but again this was initially interpreted as *post-mortem* scalp change. However, fracturing of the skull was later confirmed by xeroradiography.

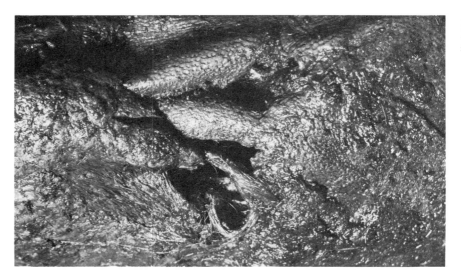

12 Close-up of Lindow Man's scalp injuries, at the apex of the head.

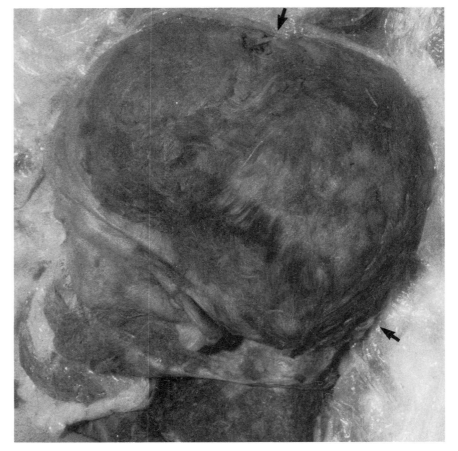

13 Infra-red photograph of the head of Lindow Man, showing not only the injury at the top but also the splitting of the skull at the back.

14 The knotted thong comes into view during the clearing away of the peat from the neck region.

In the neck region the surprises were twofold. As the brown mixed-plant debris was carefully cleaned away, it became increasingly clear that what at first sight appeared to be a piece of root around the neck was in fact a thong of sinew, 1·5 millimetres thick, made of two fibrous strands with twists and some fairly simple knots. Was this thong decorative, the equivalent in tissue of a metal torc, or was its purpose more sinister? Its circumference, 315 millimetres, is markedly smaller than normal modern collar sizes for men, and post-depositional changes in the body are unlikely to have affected this measurement greatly. In fact the thong bites deeply into the neck, as if its purpose were to choke or garrotte. Moreover, the head has an uncomfortable positioning onto one side of the chest, a posture which computer tomography (CT) scans showed to be accentuated by an abnormal angulation of the neck and two broken vertebrae, such as could be produced by strangulation or garrotting with a simultaneous heavy blow or forward dragging action to the back of the head. The twisting of the thong would also suggest that it was being used as a choking device, not as a decorative band. Indeed, there has been noticeable overtwisting, resulting in four 'backspins' distributed at the front and back of the neck.

The knot in the thong was closely studied by Geoffrey Budworth, one of the forensic specialists. The first question was whether the knot was of a special kind, perhaps even one not normally in use today. On this point, however, we were disappointed, although it should be said that, without loosening and untying it, it is possible that a subtle finer detail of the knot could have been missed. The knot as a whole comprises three separate overhand or thumb knots close together. In other words, there are stopper knots at each end of the cord, and a third knot linking both ends. Such is the specialist nature of knot studies, that the twisting can be shown to helix clockwise; that is, the knots are 'right-handed' (although they could still have been made by a left-handed person!).

15 Geoffrey Budworth, the knot expert, demonstrates the simple nature of the Lindow knots.

The extremely short ends of the knots are puzzling, and one end is somewhat frayed. Why, if the cord was for execution purposes, were they made so neat and tidy? Has the frayed end a story to tell? Could it be that an attempted garrotting resulted in a broken cord and that a 'tidying-up' operation followed, producing a short, tourniquet-like band round the neck? On the other hand, if this cord was essentially of ritual value, to control the flow of blood from the cut neck, then perhaps there was pride of workmanship even in this sordid task? Perhaps one should remember here that in the Middle Ages, and even earlier, knots were sometimes considered to have magico-religious significance, which would no doubt also demand that they be well prepared.

Finally, an attempt was made to establish the species of the tissue used. Ann Priston of the Metropolitan Police Forensic Science Laboratory took a 2 millimetre length of the cord, and after overnight extraction with 4% ammonia, the extract was tested (by electrophoresis) against anti-sera from cow, horse, humans, deer, pig and sheep. Sadly, no positive results were obtained.

By now there seemed little doubt that some of these features at least were evidence of 'overkill' – the sort of violence which perhaps made sense as part of a complex ritual but seemed extravagant as a straightforward act of murder. But there was a second puzzle in the neck area. When an attempt was made to ease the chin gently up off the chest and to look at the front of the neck and the concealed part of the thong, it was seen that the throat appeared to be slit on the right side. Was this again *post-mortem* stretching and splitting? This has been debated by various members of the investigating team, but the most likely explanation, supported by Dr West, is that the straightness and length of the lesion indicates a cut into the throat, presumably to draw blood. It was suggested that its purpose was to

16 The cut throat of Lindow Man, seen in a mirror, The slit was not easy to see, as it was obscured by the lower jaw resting on the right shoulder.

bleed the victim rather than to kill him, because it seems quite unnecessary to have committed so many alternative forms of violence in order to take his life. If the individual had been rendered unconscious by the heavy and damaging blows to the upper head, even garrotting would have been something of an optional extra, and slitting the throat completely superfluous unless blood had to be spilled in some way for symbolic reasons.

Although this appears, on the evidence of the injuries alone, to be the most complex example of 'overkill' seen in any bog body, Grauballe Man had similar multiple injuries. The bodies from Borre Fen (at least one woman and a man) and from Rendswühren Fen also had injuries extending over more than one part of the body (Table 2). Although it is now impossible to be sure that some of these injuries

Table 2
Some evidence of injury in Danish and other European bog bodies, compared with Lindow Man

Beheading	Asphyxia (Hanging and Strangulation)	Throat Cut	Skull Injuries	Other Fractures	Chest Wound	
	x					Tollund Man
	x		x			Borre Fen Man
		x	x	x		Grauballe Man
			x		x	Rendswühren Fen Man
x			x			Osterby Man
			x	x		Borre Fen Woman (II)
			x			Borre Fen Woman (III)
	x					Elling Woman
	x					Lykkegard Man
x						Stidsholt Fen Woman
					x	Werdingerveen Man
	x	x	x		x?	LINDOW MAN

did not occur at a later date as a result of disturbance of the corpses, it seems more likely that most of the injuries described on bog bodies did in fact happen at about the time of death. In most cases, we can be reasonably certain that the bodies had lain undisturbed in their peaty graves since their initial deposition and that their discovery by peat diggers did not cause injuries which were misinterpreted as original. Where damage of this kind did occur, such as the removal of a foot and a hand from the Windeby body during peat cutting, this was obvious enough. We should also remember that many bog bodies which have been found have not been investigated carefully, and thus the apparent rarity of injury on other bodies may be partly a reflection of inadequate study.

In Table 2, the injuries in Lindow Man are compared with those noted on eleven other bog bodies. By far the most common damage appears to have resulted from blows to the head, made not by swords or axes (which would have produced well-defined incised wounds) but by relatively blunt, heavy objects. These blows must sometimes have caused unconsciousness or even death, as in Lindow Man. The most certain method of killing the victim was decapitation with a sword, and presumably those from Osterby and Stidsholt were not first injured or rendered unconscious by other means. The precise reason for the asphyxiation of Lindow Man is less easy to establish. Tollund Man had a noose of plaited skin rope around his neck, and one expert view was that this had been used to 'hang' rather than to strangle him. But although the rope had left impressions in the sides of the neck and under the chin, the neck bones were not damaged or displaced. The term 'hanging', then, does not here imply the recent British judicial form where the body was dropped some distance on the end of a noose, with consequent dislocation of the neck and rupturing of the spinal cord. Similarly, the hemp rope around the neck of the Borre Fen man could have provided a short hanging line or simply have been used to strangle him. In fact, as in Lindow Man, it could even conceivably have been used as a garrotte, had a stick been inserted and twisted.

17 The head of Grauballe Man, showing the cut throat.

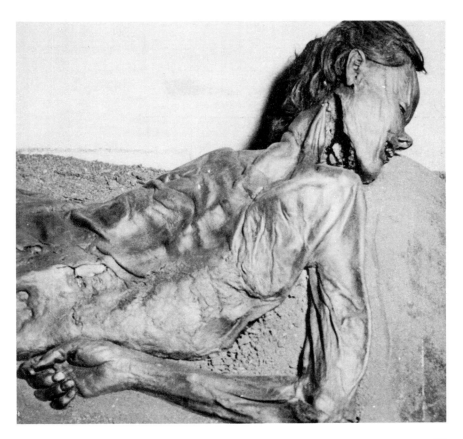

Where bog bodies display wounds made by sharp-edged cutting objects, these occur specifically in the neck and chest. The cut to the throat of Grauballe Man was long, deep and life-destroying, although he may have been rendered unconscious first. In contrast, the cut on the neck of Lindow Man is more restricted and might at most have caused much bleeding. The most problematical of all the Lindow injuries is the possible small slit wound in the chest. The bodies from Rendswühren Fen and Werdingerveen show similar injuries, suggesting stab wounds, near the heart, but the difference in Lindow Man's case is the fact that other forms of violence evident on his body would have been sufficient to kill him.

Compared with other bog bodies, therefore, Lindow Man seems to show a much wider range of injuries, several of which could independently have led to his death. It is as if almost all the methods of killing someone were encapsulated in this one individual. Did each different act of violence have some specific ritual significance?

Can a study of injuries in other ancient bodies help to unravel this mystery? Unfortunately, evidence of violence from other types of ancient site does not add very much to that found in the bog bodies, and is usually of a different kind. Beheading is seen in early British and other European skeletal material, but is uncommon, and there is little evidence of hanging or strangulation, although this has been suggested in a few instances. While cutting the throat has been fairly common during the past century, in both suicide and homicide, archaeological evidence of this is mainly restricted to bog bodies.

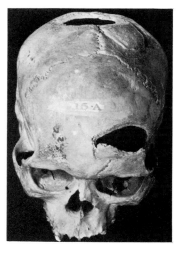

18 (*above*) Ancient Nubian skull, showing three separate injuries, A deep sword-cut in the left frontal region has caused fracturing into the orbit and a large open wound. Two further sword cuts are seen near the crown of the vault. In all cases there is healing (British Museum, Natural History).

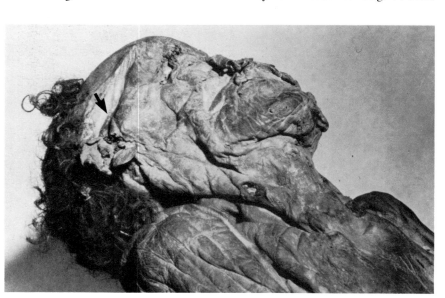

19 Right side of the head of the Guanche mummy, now in Cambridge, showing marked facial damage, possibly sustained around the time of death.

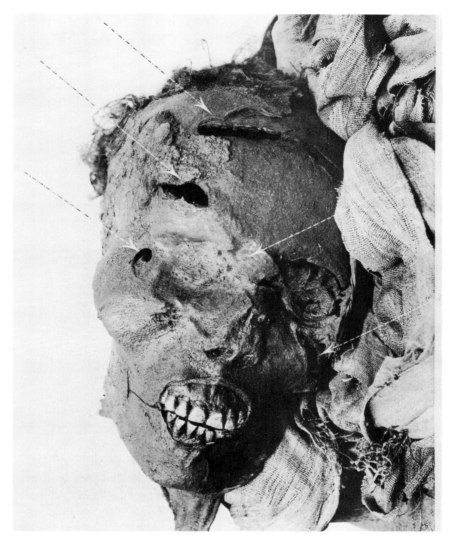

20 The head of the Egyptian king Seqenenre II. The arrows point to a series of head injuries, suggesting that he was knocked down and killed by a number of powerful blows (Cairo Museum).

Chest wounds are rare, although healed fractured ribs occur relatively frequently in skeletal material. Although in the case of the medieval nobleman from St Bees there was no puncture injury to the external chest, internally Dr E. Tapp found a broken rib and haemorrhage into the pleural cavity (haemothorax), possibly from a tear in the right lung – a sequence of events which led to death.

In ancient skeletons one of the most common areas to show injury is the head, where quite extensive damage to the bones, followed by healing, has often been noted. There are also numerous examples of bones marked by axe or sword cuts. But the lesson to be learned from

Lindow Man is that while we give due attention to other forms of bone damage, we tend in general to underestimate the significance of broken heads in excavated skeletons. The reason, of course, is that it is by no means easy to distinguish bones broken in life from breakage and collapse of the skull following burial and decay. This includes the jaws, and one is reminded that the St Bees nobleman, like Lindow Man, had a broken jaw suggestive of a blow to the face in life rather than rough handling after death. A similar problem arose in connection with the ancient Guanche mummy from the Canary Islands, now in Cambridge. In that case, a large area of the face and right side of the head was 'stove in' and the nature of the breakage to the bones suggested serious trauma at or just after death, when the bone was still relatively 'fresh' (that is, was not yet old and more fragile).

Hairs and Nails

Human body hair and nails, like rhino horn, are built out of a strong complex protein called keratin. It is thus not surprising that these tough structures have survived well at a variety of archaeological sites throughout the world, both arid and boggy, and even occasionally in the humid tropics. They may be found in the form of human remains, other animal debris or ornamentation, or as textiles and clothing. From the Danish Bronze Age site of Borum Eshøj has come a 'family' of oak coffin burials, the bodies of which were variously clothed in woollen garments, and from the Pazyryk tombs of Siberia we have examples of head-dresses, stockings, decorative swan figures, saddle covers, rugs and blankets, skilfully made from wool and felt. From a late Roman gypsum-filled lead coffin in Dorchester emerged the skeleton of a young man with head hair and a pigtail. Trace element studies of the hair revealed the puzzling occurrence of mercury (possibly of dietary or cosmetic origin). The pigtail was not a Roman hair-style, and, like the plaited and knotted hair of the bog man from Osterby, it might indicate a pre-Roman tribal custom.

21 The Osterby skull, its hair tied in a 'Swabian knot' (Schleswig, Schloss Gottorf).

In the New World plentiful examples of hair (and indeed nails) have been found at various sites. A separate human hair wig was discovered at Ventana Cave, Arizona, and a well-made wig of human hair was actually on the head of a 5,000-year-old body from Quiani in Chile. The early pre-Columbian bodies were sometimes dressed in clothing and wraps of very variable quality, from coarse shirts to richly decorated caps, headbands and 'ponchos'. Cotton and other plant fibres were used, but also the fine wool of the South American camelids – llama, alpaca, guanaco and vicuna.

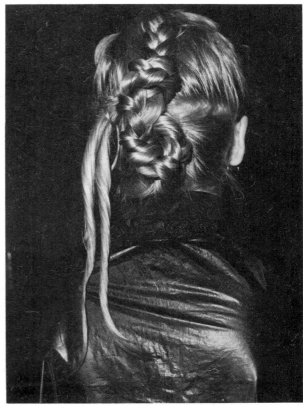

22 Back view of the Elling
Woman, partly covered in a
sheepskin cloak. Note the
'hanging furrow' around her
neck (Silkeborg Museum).

23 The Elling Woman's
hairstyle demonstrated on a
living model. The hair was
long, braided into a three-
strand plait on top, then
into seven switches at the
back, twisted and braided
together back into a large
three-stranded plait. The
plait was then wound twice
around itself to keep it out
of the way at the ritual
hanging.

The hair on Lindow Man was of three kinds. While he had little
body hair generally, there was plenty on the face and head, although it
was trimmed relatively short. Lindow Man is somewhat exceptional
among European finds in having a beard. On the upper part of his left
arm, there was a clear but incomplete spread of short ginger hair, as if
from a decayed fur armband. Careful study of this by Ann Priston
suggested that it had indeed been a decorative armband of fox-fur.
Finally, while the moustache was being studied, it was noted that a
fine hair belonging to a smaller mammal had got caught up in it. It is
not possible to be sure of the identity of this one hair, and although it
may simply have drifted off the armband, it could equally well be a
hair breathed up onto the face while skinning or handling an animal.

The head hair was fragile but generally in good shape, although
there were some patches of erosion. In general, however, the original
outer cuticular scales could still be seen, and in contrast to some
mummy hair, there was no evidence of fungal damage. The head hair
was brown to ginger in colour, and the beard a little darker. Was the

35

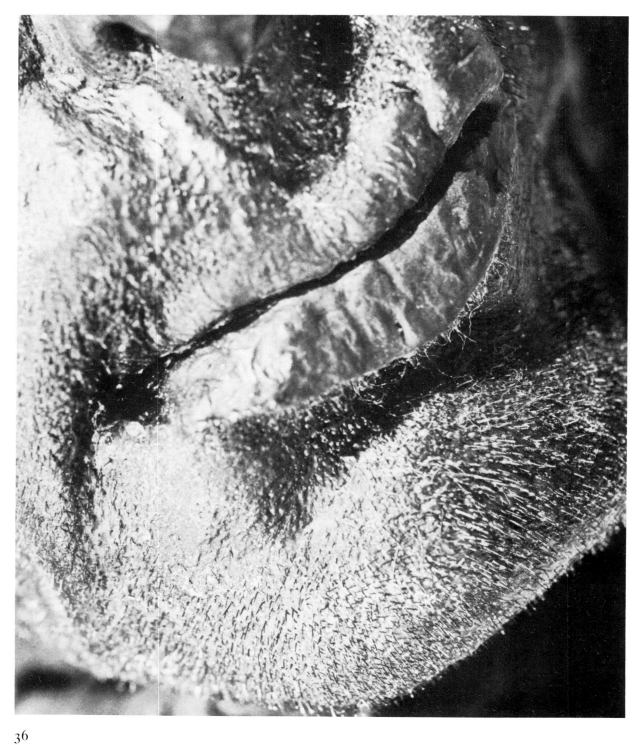

24 (*left*) The chin of Tollund Man, with a hair growth of two or three days' duration.

25 Close-up of a small mammal hair caught on a larger eroded facial hair from Lindow Man.

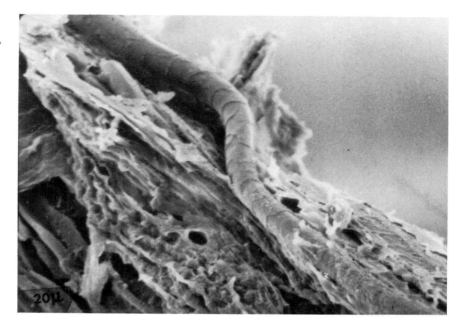

ginger appearance natural? Dr Priston checked a specimen for possible dye, but, as expected, the results were negative. In fact archaeological hair is often ginger in colour, and this seems to indicate not an ancient world of red-heads but *post-mortem* chemical changes in the pigment (eumelanin).

Another question arose when the facial hair was cleaned and could be viewed closely. The moustache appeared to be badly trimmed, and indeed there was even evidence of some 'notching'. What sort of instrument had been used for the barbering, and would high-magnification viewing of the cut hair ends provide useful clues? One or two hairs were carefully plucked from a cut area and, together with some modern comparative specimens, were submitted to close study under the scanning electron microscope (SEM). It became evident that some of the hair ends displayed a stepped appearance. An experimental study of modern hair cutting methods showed differences in the appearance of the hair ends: while a razor sheared through the hair (sometimes rather obliquely), scissors or shears produced a step effect. In fact, scissors appear to have been introduced into Britain only after the Roman period, and shears were not a common personal item in the pre-Roman Iron Age. Nevertheless, the hair notching and the microscopic stepping effect of the hair ends establish satisfactorily that Lindow Man was sufficiently privileged to have access to shears only a few days before his death.

37

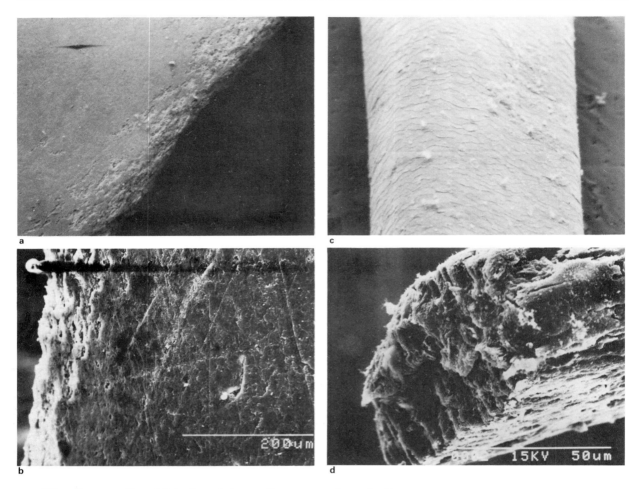

The fingernails of Lindow Man tell a somewhat similar story. When they were first uncovered and cleaned, their most striking feature was their 'polished' and 'manicured' appearance. Were these the nails of a man whose life was rough – a person intimately linked to labours on the land? One's immediate impression was that they were more like the nails of a bank clerk, perhaps belonging to someone with the sheltered status of a tribal leader or dignitary. Again the scanning electron microscope was brought into use, and again modern specimens were obtained for comparison, including nails from a 'housewife', a teacher and an agricultural worker, as well as from a medieval Irish bog woman.

Under the SEM, the Lindow nail end was seen to be remarkably rounded, and it certainly had not been trimmed for some time before death. Moreover, the surface generally displayed relatively few

26 Nails and hair of Lindow Man: (a) low magnification of smooth nail end; (b) higher magnification showing some fine scratches; (c) detail of general surface of hair (cuticular scales); (d) high magnification of cut end of hair, showing 'step' effect.

scratches at higher magnification, and in this respect contrasted markedly with that of the agricultural worker. In the latter, there were numerous deep scratches criss-crossing the surface, but mainly running parallel to the working edge. There was also some contrast between the Lindow nail and that of the Irish bog woman; in particular, her nail end was not neatly cut, but was chipped and a little broken.

Surprisingly, there is little published information to compare these results with, and it would be interesting if other nails could now be studied in more detail. Grauballe Man's fingernails do not look as smooth as those of Lindow Man, but they may have been affected by drying and conservation techniques. It may be significant that the specialists who examined his fingerprints considered that he too had the hands of a person who did not do manual work. If we were now to study the well-preserved nails of the Greenlandic people of Qilakit-soq, would we find the buffing effect of handling skins, or ice 'scratches' on them? And what of the long and intact nails on some Peruvian mummies? As so often happens in bio-archaeological investigations, initial questions open up whole new areas for future research.

27 Two of the fingernails of the St Bees man, showing the relatively smooth and rounded surfaces similar to those of Lindow Man.

The King who Wore no Clothes?

As far as one can detect, Lindow Man had been left naked except for a fox-fur armband and a thong about his neck. Why? Was this an ancient mugging where even his clothes were of value and thus stolen? Taking into account all the other pre-Saxon bog bodies from Europe, this simple mugging analogy with our own times does not seem satisfactory.

To begin with, was there in fact any evidence of clothing? There were certainly no skins or textiles near the body, at least not in the remaining area of peat which could be excavated carefully. Woollens would have preserved well and could not have been missed, and even fabrics made of plant fibres should have been stained but recognisable. Might Lindow Man have been 'wearing' the thinnest of all body coverings, woad? In case the peat staining was obscuring evidence of woad or other dyes, the body underwent infra-red photography, but with negative results. It was also possible that body dye might have migrated onto the contacting surfaces of the surrounding peat, and relevant peat samples were therefore tested by G. W. Taylor for dyes, including indigotin (woad colouring), but all results were again negative.

The body was therefore nearly naked, and we are left pondering whether this man was a king or a pauper. The state of his fingernails suggests that he was not a labourer, farmer or craftsman, but can we narrow down any of the other alternatives? If we consider the various bog bodies found throughout Europe, a number of facts emerge which may well be pertinent to the eventual understanding of Lindow Man and the circumstances of his death. First of all, there seems to be a marked difference between the extent of dress or undress on medieval and post-medieval bodies and those which are earlier. For instance, medieval bodies from Skjoldehamn in Norway and Bocksten in Denmark were clothed. A seventeenth-century body from Tawnamore in Ireland was very well dressed, in mainly woollen clothes, with felt hat, greatcoat, well-cut jacket, breeches, knitted woollen stockings, and shoes of untanned hide. Roughly contemporary are three Scottish bodies from Barrock in Caithness, Gunnister in Shetland and Arnish Moor in Lewis. These wore more modest woollen outfits, characteristic of the ordinary people of northern Britain (Plate III). In most cases, these bodies probably came to be in the bog purely by accident, although foul play or unusual reasons for burial there cannot be completely ruled out.

In the case of earlier bog bodies, the contrast is striking. Where there is clothing, it is usually incomplete and sometimes dishevelled

28 Back view of the Borre Fen III woman, with clothing drawn to one side. The head region is severely damaged and decayed (Copenhagen, National Museum).

or even placed by the side of the corpse. The plump Borre Fen III woman from Denmark (c. 770 BC) lay face down in the bog, naked except for a voluminous woollen skirt, which at the front covered her trunk up to the armpits, while at the back it was dragged up to the lower part of her head, leaving the right buttock exposed. The Borre Fen II woman also had crumpled clothing – a drape and a long, fringed shawl – placed over her naked body. There was nothing unusual in the style of her dress, which was probably a fairly typical Iron Age costume, but the arrangement of the clothing was puzzling. Could it also be significant that close by her were the remains of a new-born baby? The woman had short, cropped hair and appeared to have suffered some violence, as her right leg was fractured. One is reminded of the writings of Tacitus (c. AD 55–c. 120), the Roman politician and historian, on the question of adultery among the

41

contemporary Germanic peoples: 'A guilty wife is summarily pun-
ished by her husband. He cuts off her hair, strips her naked, and in the
presence of kinsmen turns her out of his house and flogs her all
through the village.' Was Borre Fen II a case of over-zealous and
violent retribution?

The Huldre Fen woman (AD 95) was another exception, with a
quantity of clothing, including a lambskin cape, a checked skirt and
head-scarf. These, together with an attractive horn comb and a string
with two amber beads, are strongly indicative of a person of high
social rank. But besides these clothed bodies, there are many which
were not. Grauballe Man was naked, and Tollund Man had only a cap
and belt. The first body found at Borre Fen, a man, was completely
naked except for a rope around his neck. What, then, does all this add
up to? Few of the earlier bodies were properly clothed, and many were
naked. Some showed evidence of violence, and a few were staked
down into the bog, a somewhat eerie fact which may have had ritual
significance but could equally well have been intended simply to

29 (*left*) Woollen drape
found on the Borre Fen II
woman (Copenhagen,
National Museum).

30 Fringed shawl found on
the Borre Fen II woman
(Copenhagen, National
Museum).

31 The head of Tollund
Man, wearing his sheepskin
cap, which was fastened
under the chin.

42

ensure that the body did not float to the surface in a pool. In some cases the hair was noticeably short, if not actually cropped. While there may be separate and specific reasons for some bog burials, can the rest be seen in more general cultural terms as indications of ritual sacrifice or the result of punishment and execution? It is extremely difficult from the standpoint of our own society late in the twentieth century to project ourselves back in time and make an unbiased interpretation of the facts. But perhaps Tacitus may help again here:

'Traitors and deserters', he says of northern tribes, 'are hanged on trees; cowards, shirkers and sodomites are pressed down under a wicker hurdle into the slimy mud of a bog.' Drowning is referred to in connection with the rituals of tribal groups in the Danish area. Commenting on the worship of Nerthus, Mother Earth, Tacitus says that after a festival, 'the chariot, vestments, and ... the goddess herself, are cleansed in a secluded lake. This service is performed by slaves who are immediately afterwards drowned in the lake.' Was there some equivalent ritual which could use the pools in bogs? Again, as regards rituals, we are told, 'above all other gods they worship Mercury, and count it no sin, on certain feast-days, to include human victims in the sacrifices offered to him.' Other observations in Tacitus's writings also show that human sacrifices still occurred in some parts of Europe as late as Roman times.

Much sifting and sorting of the evidence on bog bodies, including Lindow Man, continues. His nakedness and his unusual range of injuries not only relate him to other early bog bodies, but surely also give strength to the argument that there was a ritual element in his treatment and death. This is also suggested by some of the evidence from his gut, discussed fully in Chapter 6. Moreover, why did he have a well-developed, but roughly trimmed, beard – unique among bog bodies – and well-kept nails? Was he an aristocrat fallen on hard times, or a high-born prisoner sacrificed to the gods?

3. Reconstructing a Physique

How tall was Lindow Man? Was he robust and muscular? Such questions of physique may seem difficult to resolve when only a skeleton is available, as it must be 'clothed' in soft tissues in order to evaluate its owner's size and shape; but one might imagine that when a body is relatively intact answers would be more easily forthcoming. Sadly, this is not so. The legs of Lindow Man were cut away, and so we do not have the full length of his body. Also his posture, especially in the head and neck region, is distorted, and thus it is not even easy to arrive at a precise head and trunk length. In terms of robustness, there has been a flattening and splaying out of the soft tissues in the region of the chest and arms, giving a somewhat false impression of breadth and muscular strength. There is also the possibility that the body suffered some *post-mortem* bloating while immersed in a boggy pool, although I believe the 'normal' appearance of the face argues against this.

In spite of these problems, Lindow Man does give the overall impression of being well built. Exactly how tall he was is a matter of some debate. In the case of skeletal remains, it is usual to evaluate stature from the lengths of one or more main long bones. The two large leg bones (femur and tibia) give the most accurate results, but others can be used provided it is remembered that the height estimate may be slightly less accurate. In the case of Lindow Man, we had no leg measurements, but an upper arm bone (humerus) could be used. During cleaning, the upper and lower extremities of the humerus were tentatively found by means of marker needles, and from these a maximum length of 330 millimetres was obtained. By applying a stature regression formula to this measurement, it was possible to obtain an idea of the original full standing height of Lindow Man. This formula was worked out on a sample of Europeans, where both stature and individual bone measurements were available. The metrical relationships (regressions) of bone lengths to full body lengths could thus be established. For the humerus, the formula used was $2 \cdot 89$ ($\times$ humerus length in centimetres) $+ 78 \cdot 10$. Thus

$2 \cdot 89 \times 33 \cdot 0 + 78 \cdot 10 = 173 \cdot 47$ centimetres (5 ft $8\frac{1}{4}$ in). Robert Connolly, who undertook a careful separate evaluation of the physique, arrived at a slightly smaller stature of 168 centimetres (5 ft 6 in). Even allowing for this variation in estimates of stature, Lindow Man would be of fairly average height in Britain today, although he may have been a little taller than many of his Celtic contemporaries.

Beyond Photography – Contouring the Body

Lindow Man has been much photographed since his discovery. During the early stages of excavating and cleaning the body in the laboratory, many photographs were taken to provide a record of the proceedings. The body was also filmed for a 'Q.E.D.' television documentary. Finally, the Terrestrial Photogrammetry Unit of the

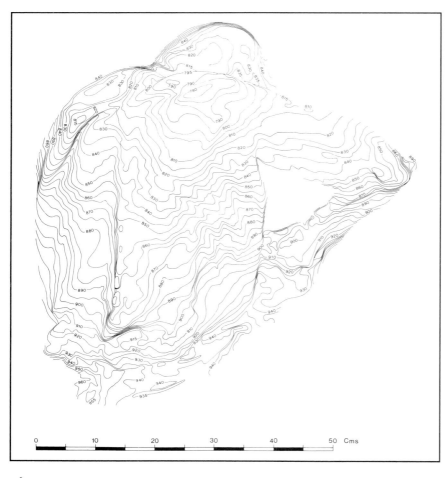

32 Detailed contouring of the body of Lindow Man, obtained by photo-grammetric methods: back view.

City University took a series of photographs in 'stereo-pairs' to enable accurate measurement and contouring of the body to be carried out. Over the past three decades this 'contour-mapping' procedure has been applied to the study of variation in humans, using a number of different techniques. The result can be a sensitive and precise evaluation of differences in shape, ranging from details such as individual teeth to whole heads or bodies. The method clearly has considerable potential, and it is surprising that it has not been applied before to ancient human remains. In the 'contour map' we have a valuable record of the shape and size of the Lindow body just after its excavation from the peat, before drying or other changes could take place and before freeze-drying was undertaken. This record will be of considerable benefit to the scientists responsible for the long-term conservation and preservation of Lindow Man.

33 'Contour map' of Lindow Man: front view.

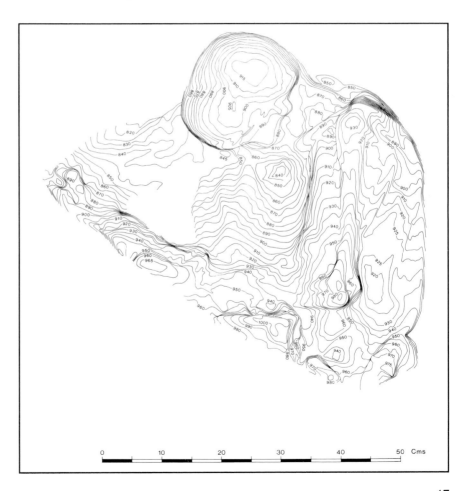

47

Transforming the Face

In the latter part of the nineteenth century, scientists and artists became intrigued by the possibility of clothing the dry bones of a head or body in flesh, in order to get a more realistic impression of what the people of the past looked like. This included attempts to reconstruct fossil man from the few recognised finds at that time. Methods gradually become more scientific, and eventually thicknesses of muscle and other tissue were carefully assessed in order to make reconstruction more precise. The biggest problem, especially in older adults, is of course to determine reliably the amount of fat on the face or under the chin.

Although much caution is needed, such reconstructions have at times produced some useful corroborative evidence for forensic

34 (*above*) A very early reconstruction of an ancient head, in this case of Neanderthal man, from the 'Manual of the Antiquity of Man', published in 1879.

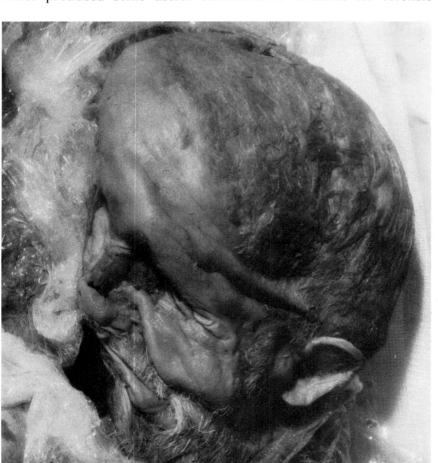

35 Infra-red photograph of the face of Lindow Man. The torn skin over the nose can be seen, as well as the closed left eyelid and the lips. The left ear is only slightly distorted. Some of the injuries to the top of the head are also visible.

scientists wishing to check refleshed bones against portraits of murdered individuals. In the field of anthropology and archaeology the subject received special attention three decades ago as a result of the work of Professor Gerasimov in Russia. Most recently, scientists working on the Manchester mummy project collaborated with Richard Neave, a medical illustrator, in the reconstruction of three Egyptian mummy heads. The 'Two Brothers', Khnum-Nakht and Nekht-Ankh, were reconstructed and it was suggested that the former had somewhat negroid features, but actually the reconstructed nose does not give this impression and is a reminder of the fact that not only must differing soft tissue thicknesses be considered, but also the subtle differences in the shapes of the heads of peoples from various parts of the world. The reconstruction of Mummy 1770 produced a

36 Bringing the face to life: a reconstruction of Lindow Man based on measurement and a careful evaluation of his probable appearance before *post-mortem* changes set in.

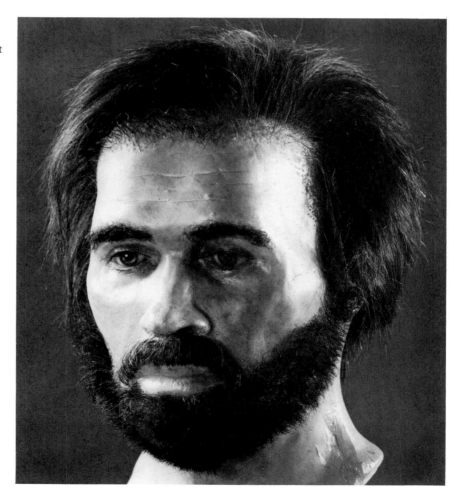

49

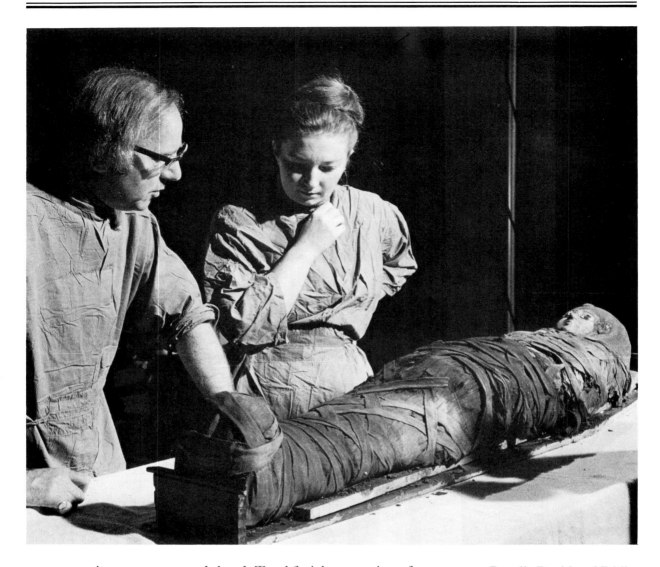

very attractive young woman's head. Total facial restoration of course means implanting glass eyes and adding eyelashes and a wig, to give a lifelike appearance.

In the case of the deformed and compressed Lindow Man, Neave was again able to apply his skills at restoration. The head bones had been decalcified, with consequent deformation. There was also some tearing of the soft tissue on the face, in the region of the nose. Much measuring and remodelling of the head and face was therefore necessary. But the result is pleasing, and gives us a far better idea of how this Iron Age Briton may have looked.

37 Rosalie David and Eddie Tapp prepare to unwrap the Egyptian mummy 1770, as part of the Manchester University new mummy project.

50

The Teeth

Teeth are among the most durable of all human tissues, and often preserve well when other human remains are much decayed. Fortunately, they can provide a range of useful information. Depending on their antiquity, they may provide evidence of the level of hominid evolution or even variation within more recent peoples; they can also give information about age and aspects of health (especially as regards caries cavities and possible illness during childhood).

In the case of bog bodies there is a special snag, however. Lindow Man's teeth were studied by Denys Goose, a dental specialist. Thirty of the possible total of thirty-two teeth were found in the mouth, but the acidity of the bog water had totally removed the hard, calcified enamel caps (outer layer of the crowns). The softer inner dentine was also somewhat decalcified, but owing to its greater organic content it remained identifiable in shape. There were, however, some *post-*

38 (*below, left*) A molar of Lindow Man, showing *ante-mortem* fracture.

39 A lower molar and premolars of Lindow Man, looking unworn but in fact devoid of the outer enamel layer of the crown.

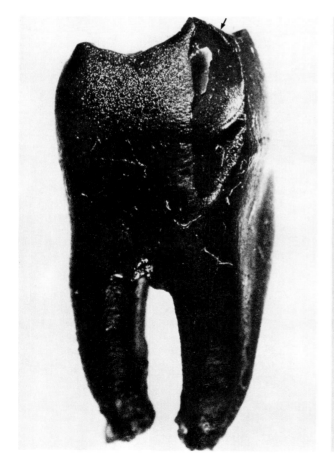

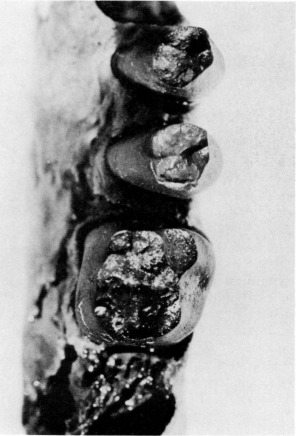

51

mortem erosions into this tissue, which an inexperienced eye could have mistaken for caries cavities.

Allowing for these limitations, some useful facts were still obtained. First, as only two were missing (and this could have happened at or after death), it looks as if Lindow Man's teeth were healthy. At least, there were no certain large caries cavities which had penetrated down to the dentine. Secondly, the shape and size of the inner dentine and roots were normal (one can find odd-shaped or reduced crowns and anomalous roots). Because day-to-day wear on the chewing surfaces of teeth gradually exposes the inner dentine, there is a chance of finding evidence of especially pronounced wear, even if the enamel has gone. Lindow Man's first molars clearly showed considerable wear, although the third molars had not changed much, suggesting an age of around 25–30 years. The lower second molar, however, had a most unusual feature: a vertical 'splinter' of tooth had sheared off and was missing. The edges of this damage were sharp and unworn, and strongly suggest that it occurred during the final violence to Lindow Man. One of the blows to the head could well have resulted in a sharp jarring together of the jaws, with a chipped tooth as a consequence. On the other hand, taken with the evidence of the broken lower jaw, could this perhaps suggest a separate blow to the lower face?

Blood Stains and Blood Groups

Since the turn of the century, there has been a growing interest in the study of blood, both at a medical and an archaeological level. Landsteiner's momentous discovery in 1901 of the first of the blood group systems, the ABO, meant that transfusions could be undertaken relatively safely for the first time. A few years later, two anatomists, Elliot Smith and Wood Jones, who were assisting in the study of human remains in Egypt and Nubia, became intrigued by apparent blood stains on them. 'This blood-staining of the bones', they wrote, 'is a diagnostic point of great value in bodies buried in Nubia. The limit of its persistence we do not know, but it is certainly very vivid upon bones the archaeological dating of which refers them to a period well over five thousand years ago.' In some cases, they were dealing with mummies rather than only skeletal remains, and they noted that, in the case of the mummy of Ramesses V, an *ante-mortem* injury to the skull was associated with a 'wide area of discolouration'. The problem, however, was to demonstrate scientifically and beyond doubt that this was blood staining, and their tests failed to do this.

40 Section through an Egyptian mummy scalp, showing numerous microstructures which may be red cells derived from blood.

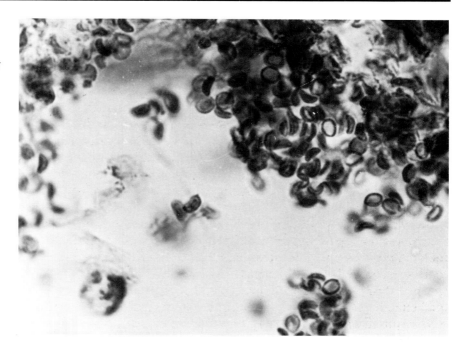

Since then, the problem has repeated itself again and again, but there have been a few interesting recent developments. Of special interest are some skeletons of old whalers at Spitzbergen, which seem to show clear evidence of localised blood stains, thought to be linked to the vitamin-deficiency disease scurvy (which can produce bone-surface haemorrhaging). Another surprise was the discovery of fresh-looking congealed red blood within the injured chest of the St Bees medieval knight (Plate IX). Under the microscope, however, changes were shown to have taken place in this fluid and the cells to have decomposed. Nevertheless, it was possible to confirm spectroscopically that it contained 'haemoglobin degeneration products'; that is, the pigment of the red blood corpuscles was still present.

At times, microscopic examination of tissue from bodies may seem to reveal actual blood corpuscles, and in some cases this is beyond doubt. Indeed, Jeanne Riddle demonstrated in a female Egyptian mummy (PUM III, *c.* 835 BC) not only the relatively tougher red corpuscles (erythrocytes) but other blood cells – neutrophils, eosinophils and lymphocytes. However, extreme caution is obviously necessary in the interpretation of such minute structures, and Dr Riddle showed that, in one case, structures that initially looked like red blood corpuscles were hollow in the middle and were in fact compressed fungal spores.

53

In the case of Lindow Man and the other European bog bodies there has seemed to be little chance of finding blood, for the heart, the blood vessels and the body fluids have usually been destroyed by decomposition processes begun before the peaty waters could bring about a halt in decay. However, recent investigations of the Borre Fen III woman have revealed clusters of red blood corpuscles in some tissue sections. During the cleaning away of the peat from the Lindow head and the discovery of the damaged scalp and compressed fracture at the crown, it appeared that the surrounding hair and peat were more darkly stained. As the injury was severe and was thought to have happened at rather than after death, it could have resulted in much bleeding. Clotted and dried blood could have been mixed and matted initially with the hair and eventually also with the peat. The nature of this residue has not yet been confirmed, but with the current development of highly sensitive techniques for the identification of minute amounts of blood it should eventually be possible. Indeed, while Lindow Man was being probed and processed, Dr Thomas Loy and his colleagues in British Columbia were engaged in the similarly difficult task of detecting blood residues on ancient stone tools. As is so often the case in science, research in one area may have a considerable pay-off in another quite different field of enquiry.

Of considerable scientific and archaeological interest, of course, is the possibility of assigning blood groups to ancient individuals. This could provide some clear-cut genetic information on past human groups, as blood groups are inherited in a simple fashion. Of the numerous types of biochemical variation which can be found in the blood, the ABO blood group system seems most likely to give stable and reliable results, although the detection of other serological variation is still a hopeful prospect for the future. Why attempt to determine such groups? There are two major reasons: first, because each person inherits a gene for A, O or B from each parent and thus may be AA, AO, AB, OO, BO or BB in the ABO blood group system, this information may help to sort out family relationships within groups of mummies or even burial clusters within cemeteries. Secondly, because frequencies for these blood group genes vary from community to community, and may well have changed radically through time, by blood-grouping substantial numbers of ancient people it should be possible to see whether such changes can be established. Theoretically, this sounds fine and exciting, but in practice there are considerable laboratory difficulties, not in basic testing procedures but in ensuring that the results are reliable, in view of the fact that burial and *post-mortem* decomposition may at times influence the nature of the blood group reactions or 'pseudo' reactions. These technical problems have been known and discussed since Drs Boyd and Boyd attempted to blood-group a series of mummies over fifty years ago. Techniques have improved, but the problems have by no means been eliminated. Nevertheless, bearing these in mind, what kinds of blood group results are available on ancient bodies, and where does Lindow Man fit into these enquiries?

Even in the pioneering researches of the Boyds, bodies rather than skeletons were investigated for possible evidence of ABO blood-group substances in the dried tissues. Their results, using a mixed group of ancient Egyptians and early Amerindians, were surprisingly promising, and of 327 individual samples, 276 reacted as group O, 37 gave A or B antigenic reactions and only 14 gave no clear grouping. Another study of 226 ancient Amerindian bodies from the Aleutian Islands, Alaska, the south-west United States and Peru, revealed far more evidence of A and B antigens than expected (about 6% of the sample). This possibility of 'picking up' evidence of micro-evolution occurring over relatively short periods of time spurred on the investigations. Thus, Dr P. C. Candela's blood-group studies of Aleut mummies were later used in a more general evaluation of the biological affinities of recent inhabitants of these islands.

The past two decades have seen a vastly expanded effort to blood-group residues in skeletons. They have also produced two especially interesting enquiries concerned with early Egyptian dignitaries. One nobleman, by the name of Nakht, who was buried at Thebes, was sufficiently well preserved to yield from a region of the brain actual red corpuscles, which gave a satisfactory group B result. Material from his spleen was also tested but, owing to heavy bacterial contamination, this gave no results at all. Of the various techniques currently being used in this kind of work, R. C. Connolly and R. D. Harrison chose the so-called serological micro-method for the investigation of kinship status between Smenkhkare and Tutankhamun. As they were physically similar and displayed the same blood group, A2, it was considered likely that there was indeed a close family relationship between them.

Much more recently, Connolly has turned his attention to a very different area from the point of view of blood-grouping – the bog body. Lindow Man is in fact the first of the bog people to be tested and to produce results. He shares his blood group, O, with the majority of people in Britain today and, judging at least by the high O group frequencies in the more 'Celtic areas' of Wales and Scotland, it seems likely that this would have been the case also in Celtic times.

4. Looking for Disease

Once the peat had been cleared away, it was possible to begin an evaluation of what remained of the Lindow body, both externally and internally. An autopsy was carried out by James Bourke, a senior surgeon with an early training in anthropology. Before any physical examination commenced, however, X-rays of the body were consulted, but owing to the decalcified state of the bones these proved to be inconclusive and limited in value. The body was therefore removed from the British Museum for additional specialised scanning by means of nuclear magnetic resonance imaging, xeroradiography and computerised tomography.

Since X-rays were discovered in the latter part of the nineteenth century, the medical world has made enormous use of the technique, but archaeology has greatly neglected it. The Egyptologist Sir

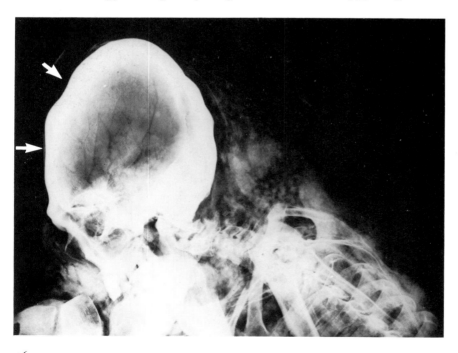

41 X-ray of part of a Peruvian 'mummy bundle', revealing a marked artificial deformity of the head.

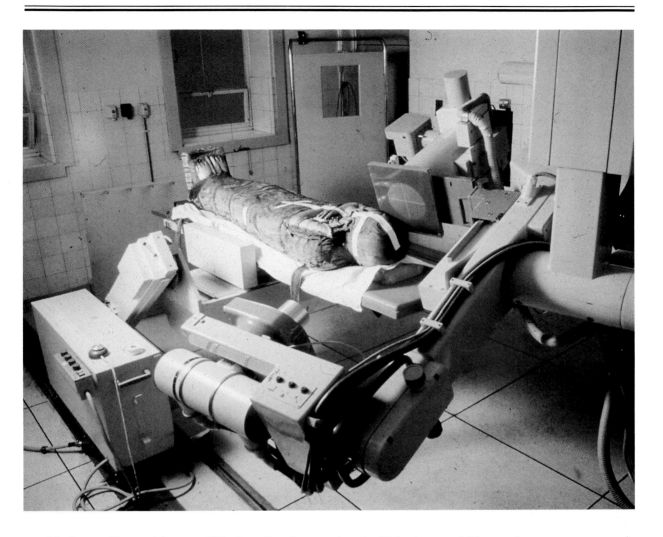

42 Modern radiographic equipment explores the body within the wrappings of mummy 1770.

Flinders Petrie was ahead of his time and X-rayed a mummy as early as 1898, but sadly few followed suit. This has now largely changed, and in recent years many bodies in various parts of the world have been X-rayed. In the case of bog bodies, however, there is a special problem. Because the acid peat may decalcify the bones to a great extent, and as these show the greatest contrast with soft tissue in the living subject, in a bog body the result is often an X-ray with little contrast between tissues. Nevertheless, some bodies, such as Grauballe Man, do display some skeletal detail. In the Lindow body, contrasts were not so good, but fortunately other techniques were more revealing.

Xeroradiography, a related technique employing selenium-

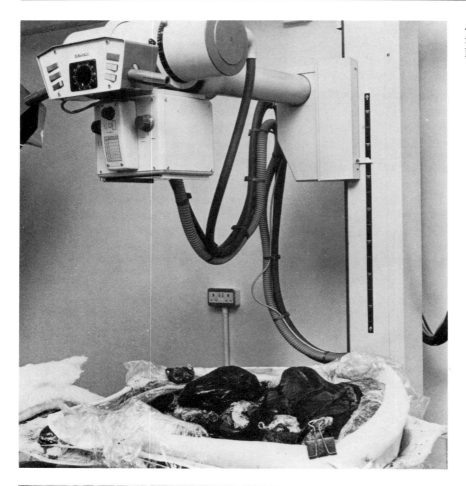

43 Lindow Man undergoing xeroradiography at the Royal Marsden Hospital.

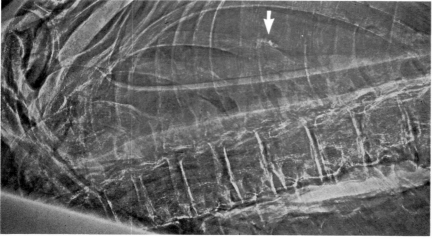

44 Xeroradiograph of part of the chest area of Lindow Man, in the region of the broken rib (arrowed).

45 An Egyptian mummy moves into the computer tomographic scanner at the Department of Diagnostic Radiology, University of Manchester.

impregnated radiographs, is better able to highlight the tissue differences in these ancient dead. The images produced by Reg Davis and colleagues at the Royal Marsden Hospital, London, were excellent and revealed some unexpected facts. Inside the brain-box, for instance, could be seen a large bone fragment which had been driven in by the injuries at the top of the head. The images also showed a meandering crack at the back of the skull, a broken rib and vertebrae – all the result of a blunt weapon or weapons.

This sensitive technique is not to be confused with nuclear magnetic resonance imaging (NMR), which is concerned with hydrogen ion mapping. Lindow Man was sent to Picker International Ltd of Wembley, who produced additional internal 'views' of the body by this method. As this imaging technique is still being improved, it may be of greater use in this context in the future.

However, where a body has been in acidic, waterlogged bog deposits for centuries and has suffered decalcification of the skeleton as a result, computerised axial tomography (CAT or CT) scanning will be the preferred technique for internal investigation. CT scanning has been of growing medical importance during two decades, and for once archaeology was quick to realise its potential. The brain of an early Egyptian was scanned in 1977 and since then

59

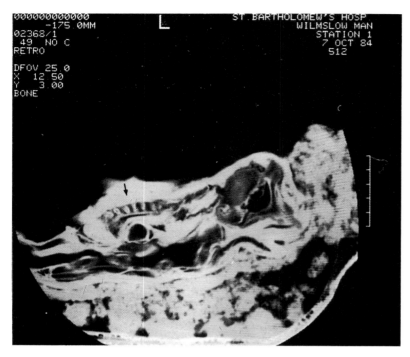

other Egyptian mummy material has been checked for inner detail by this non-destructive means.

This radio-diagnostic technique is somewhat different from conventional X-rays and does not rely on the usual radiographic film. Instead, X-ray beams penetrate the layers of the body in fine sections, rather like a bacon slicer. Indeed, the word 'tomography' is from the Greek word *tomos*, meaning a slice. The contrasts in tissues and densities are fed back into a computer. These multiple scans, at 5-millimetre intervals, can be displayed on the computer as transverse sections or reconsidered in relation to different angles or orientations.

The 100 scans obtained for Lindow Man were in some parts a disappointment and in others a revelation. The decomposed remains of his brain were clearly visible, as was the damage to the top of the head, the compressed bone fragments and a fracture to the right side of the occipital bone. Moreover, the severe angled damage to his spine in the neck region showed up very well. Quite a few of his teeth were demonstrably present, but not all of them could be accounted for by the scan.

However, by far the most impressive evidence that this technique can pick up subtle differences in inner body structure was its ability to detect, within the bones of the lower spine, bubble-like 'herniations'

46 (*left*) CT scan of the lower face of Lindow Man, showing the form of part of the lower jaw (the tooth sockets are clearly visible).

47 Decalcified, shrunken and distorted mandible from the Bog of Allan, Ireland.

deep into the bodies of a number of vertebrae. These so-called Schmorl's nodes have little clinical significance but nevertheless represent minor stress or developmental problems. As a result of the scan, they were searched for during the autopsy. By opening up the cut ends of the lower thorax, James Bourke was able to remove two lumbar vertebrae for special study. To everyone's surprise, the vertebral surfaces in the areas where the nodes had shown up displayed only slight changes. The scan had thus done its job thoroughly, having penetrated the largely decalcified bone and detected fine inner structural alterations which could well have been missed if only the dry bones of the skeleton had been available for examination.

Autopsy: Open Body 'Surgery'

The detailed information provided by this battery of highly special-ised equipment enabled the body to be opened up for autopsy with far more confidence. It should be remembered that it consisted extern-ally of the trunk, devoid of lower buttocks, pubic and genital areas and most of the legs (except the left, below the knee). In addition, the forearms were decayed, the bones squashed, and parts of the fingers cut away by the Hy-Mac machinery. An autopsy would show whether the musculature was intact and whether the organs of the thorax and chest were still available for examination. It would also provide information about the state of the head and the brain.

Superficially the body looked well built, and although the skin was somewhat flattened, the general appearance suggested a reason-ably well-nourished adult male in the prime of life. The skin was like soft leather and, except for the head and face, appeared to be relatively free of hair. The neck was sharply angled and the head slumped forwards so that the chin was pushed down by the right shoulder. The pinna of the left ear had become noticeably distorted *post mortem*, presumably by the deterioration of inner cartilage. The tip of the nose had separated from the other tissue of the face. The eyes had decayed, but the eyelids, lashes and brows remained intact. Although the lower face was distorted, it too was intact, and when the mouth and lips were opened, a somewhat reduced tongue and some loose teeth were seen. No doubt the teeth had become loose as a result of the decay of the dental ligament which normally holds them in place. All the teeth were removed from the mouth for detailed study, as already described. A fragment of the lower jaw had broken away and was separate in the mouth.

Because of the cut lower trunk, it was possible to explore the

61

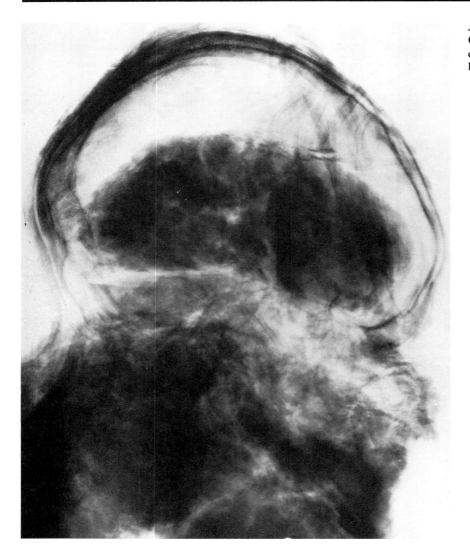

48 An X-ray of the head of Grauballe Man, showing the compact and much reduced brain at the base.

interior of the main body area without making any incisions. In fact, the anterior and posterior walls of the abdomen separated easily and could be held open. Looking up the trunk, it became clear that most of the internal tissue had decayed, but by great good fortune part of the upper alimentary tract – stomach, duodenum and jejunum – remained, and, better still, it contained the partly digested residue of the last food eaten by Lindow Man. On removal, the gut tissue was found to be very thin, owing to *post-mortem* changes, and, histologically, Bourke found that although collagen remained, actual cell detail was poor.

62

Examination of the body was facilitated by the use of an endoscope. This important piece of clinical apparatus, which makes internal examinations possible without any additional openings being made in the body, had already been used in the study of Egyptian mummies at Manchester Museum. It is an invaluable tool in the exploration of an individual prior to any surgery and it was therefore natural that James Bourke should arrange to use it on Lindow Man. Essentially, it consists of a flexible metal tube with a cold light source at the viewing end. Visual information on the tissues immediately in front of the light source is transmitted back along the curved tube and can be viewed externally. By this means, the interior of Lindow Man's mouth, throat, chest and head could be explored. The endoscope passed a little way into the throat, but came to a constriction at the level of the broken neck. This compression was so complete that peaty water could not have passed down into the stomach by this route and contaminated the contents of the gut. It was therefore possible to carry out a full study of Lindow Man's last meal (see Chapter 6).

The endoscope was also to prove invaluable in assessing the condition of the brain. As a result of the blow to the top of the head and the splitting of the scalp in this area, the endoscope tube could be passed into the head by this route. What looked like a much shrunken brain had already been revealed by the CT scan, but the actual state of this tissue was not known. While in the Windeby Girl the brain had been in a remarkably good condition, in Grauballe Man it was much reduced in size and positioned towards the base of the skull. This proved to be the case also in Lindow Man. In fact, the endoscope showed that no clear brain structure remained, and presumably the cranial injury and damage to the scalp had allowed microbes to enter the head and initiate decay. All that now remained of the brain, therefore, was a putty-like mass of altered tissue.

The Evidence for Disease

Although there could be no doubt that Lindow Man met a violent end, whether for ritual or other reasons, it was still useful to examine the body for signs of disease. As well as the full autopsy examination, the surface of the body was studied for evidence of skin changes and swelling, while the X-rays and internal scanning techniques allowed deeper tissues to be non-destructively investigated. A search was made for larger external parasites, fleas and lice (none were found) and the remnants of the intestinal tract were scanned microscopically for worm eggs.

A great deal has been learnt about disease in ancient man from such examinations. Early this century, Sir Grafton Elliot Smith and colleagues had examined numerous Egyptian and Nubian mummies and found evidence of various diseases. A Coptic body from Nubia, dating from the sixth century AD, showed the deformity of the hands and feet characteristic of advanced leprosy. The body of a priest of Amun (Twenty-first Dynasty, *c.* 1085–945 BC) showed changes typical of another destructive condition which was all too common in the past: a serious tuberculous infection of the spine had caused collapse of some of the bones and the resulting development of a humpback. An elderly man, possibly a foreign Christian who had settled near the temple of Philae, suffered from gout. His feet in particular, and especially his great toes, showed characteristic changes, with large white concretions which were probably a mixture of fibrous tissue and urate crystals. The mummy of a woman of the Byzantine period showed soft tissue changes within the abdomen which were interpreted as the consequence of appendicitis. The body

49 (*below*) The mummy of a Twenty-first Dynasty priest from Egypt, with clear evidence of spinal tuberculosis (abscessing, vertebral collapse and spinal deformity).

50 The young Egyptologist Margaret Murray and colleagues in 1906, at the time of unwrapping one of the 'Two Brothers', Egyptian mummies in Manchester University.

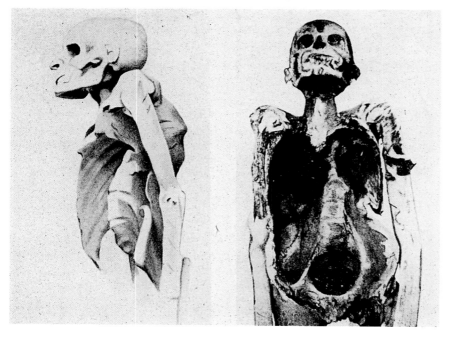

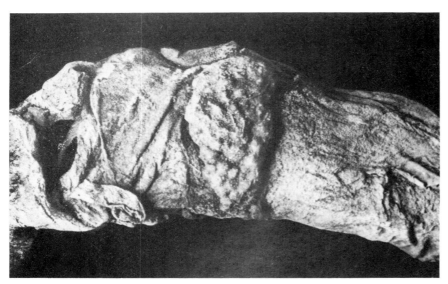

of Nekht Ankh, one of the famous Two Brothers (Twelfth Dynasty, *c.* 1991–1786 BC) now in Manchester University, was not in good condition when unwrapped, but histological studies on the soft tissue of the inner chest after rehydration showed that he had suffered from pleurisy of a lung and inflammation of the covering of the heart (pericarditis), both probably developments from an attack of pneumonia.

Samples of internal tissue from the Cambridge Guanche mummy were also rehydrated, and the investigators were surprised to find that the individual had suffered from the 'industrial disease' anthracosis, resulting from the long-term breathing of polluted air. In this particular case the carbon particles were indicative of smoke and poorly ventilated housing.

Material from the New World also provides a wealth of evidence of ancient disease, not only from numerous skeletons of early Amerindians, but also from preserved bodies. A flexed 'Basketmaker' body from the dry environment of the Canyon del Muerto in Arizona had a large *ante-mortem* hernia, which could have been caused by an accident some months or even years before death. Ruptures are in fact not uncommon in the Third World today, and it is thus not surprising that other Amerindian cases are known. In the preserved bodies of two Atacamena Indians from northern Chile (third and sixteenth centuries AD), defects in the diaphragm had allowed the intrusion of parts of the intestinal tract into the thoracic cavity.

Although it is not easy to assess the comparative frequency of gallstones, arising from gall-bladder disease, in different peoples, it seems very likely on present evidence that Amerindians are especially susceptible to the condition. The presence of two cases in seventy-five pre-Columbian bodies from northern Chile (3%) demonstrates that it may have been relatively common in antiquity as well.

Malfunction of the thyroid gland (hypothyroidism) was confirmed in a young adult Peruvian female of the Nasca culture (*c*. 90 BC), on the evidence of calcified areas of the gland and other histological changes. Finally, one can demonstrate that a Latin American condition, Carrión's disease, caused by the fly-borne microbe *Bartonella bacilliformis*, had a substantial history in the Peruvian area. It appears in another Nasca body as verruga (multiple skin lesions), and the relevant micro-organisms were tentatively identified under the scanning electron microscope.

This brief review of some of the evidence could be considerably expanded but is sufficient to show the wide range of diseases that can be identified in ancient bodies. We can now view the evidence for disease in Lindow Man against the background of these studies in what might be called 'whole body palaeopathology' as opposed to 'skeletal palaeopathology'.

The Suspected Skin Disease

The surface of Lindow Man's body looked quite normal over the chest and abdomen, but when the back was exposed, it was something of a surprise to see areas of lumpiness looking rather like very restricted and closely packed smallpox reactions. Clearly, these demanded close investigation. The specialist work of studying the skin surface was undertaken by Dr R. J. Hay, a consultant in dermatology. He found that while most of the surface looked smooth and unchanged, there had in fact been decomposition and loss of much of the thin outer layer, the epidermis. The skin also showed clear *post-mortem* changes at a microscopic level, with collagen fibres present but elastic fibres missing. Fungal hyphae, evidence of the growth and channelling of fungus into the tissue, were also found. As far as the 'lumpy rash' on the back was concerned, there was nothing to indicate true disease, but Dr Hay did find some slight difference in the arrangement of the collagen fibres, suggesting a limited *post-mortem* change. Decay can be patchy even in the skeleton, and it is not uncommon to find within a single cemetery that some areas of bone are more eroded and damaged than others, owing to minor differences in the material surrounding the bodies. Therefore, the changes in the skin of Lindow Man must be put into the category of pseudo-pathology, that is, false evidence of disease resulting from distorting *post-mortem* changes.

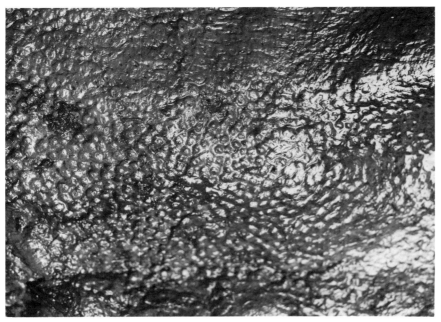

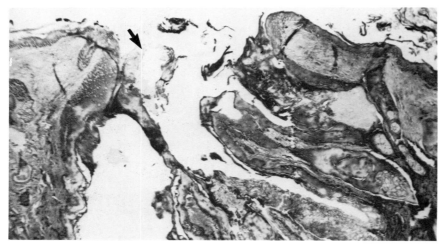

52 (*top*) Close-up of a region of the lower back of Lindow Man, showing *post-mortem* changes which look like skin disease.

53 Acne in an elderly Egyptian male mummy, with inflammation and destruction of tissue in the central part of the skin section (× 200).

54 The back of Lindow Man, fully cleaned. Impressions of some of the ribs are clearly seen, as well as the neural spines of the vertebrae. The arrow indicates the area shown in Fig. 52.

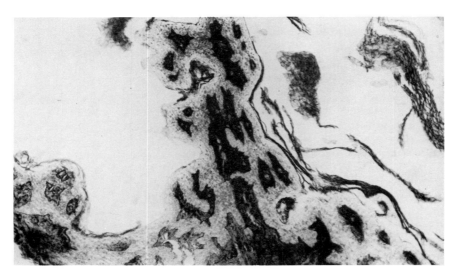

55 Section through the skin of a mummy hand, showing the growth of a small simple tumour (papilloma) (× 150).

The examination of the skin of archaeological bodies has a long history. Sir Marc Armand Ruffer undertook such studies on early Egyptians over seventy years ago. In particular, he found that the skin of hands and feet was often especially well preserved. Peruvian dried bodies and North-American cliff-dwelling Amerindians were also investigated around that time, and in 1959 the electron microscope was introduced to assist in this area of research. In a few cases, scientists have found probable evidence of true skin disease. Thus, the head of the Egyptian pharaoh Ramesses V displayed an eruption suggestive of smallpox, and Ramesses IV appeared to have true ulcers on two areas of his body.

'Rheumatism', or Diseases of the Joints

Few of us with aches and pains in our joints realise that these are not the result of one single disease. In actual fact, arthropathies, or joint diseases, are a complex and problematical series of conditions, some more closely related than others. Although certain forms can affect children, most rheumatic diseases do not begin or take effect until well into adulthood. In an advanced state, various such diseases can be detected on X-rays, and the dry bones of a skeleton can show tell-tale changes at the joints, such as 'lipping' and other modifications to joint margins. Alternatively, the actual surface of the joint may show degeneration and deformity. It is something of an enigma that rheumatoid arthritis, which is relatively common today, and another condition, true ankylosing spondylitis, appear to be of quite recent origin. At least, archaeology has not yet produced much evidence of

56 The mummified head of the pharaoh Ramesses V, showing a skin eruption which some believe to be evidence of smallpox (Cairo Museum).

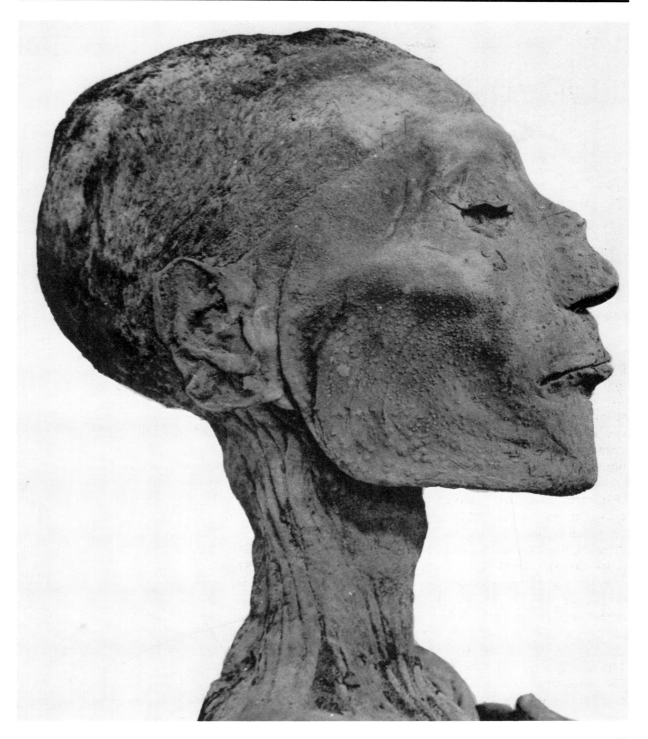

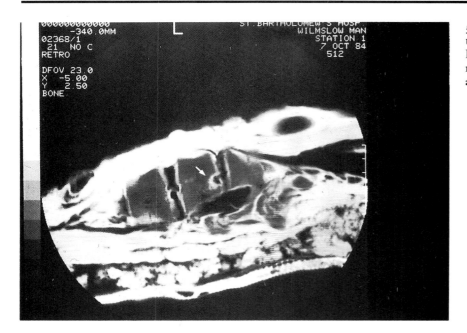

57 Computer tomograph of the abdominal region of Lindow Man, showing the minor spinal defects known as Schmorl's nodes.

them, although other joint diseases have been noted in mummies, other preserved bodies and large numbers of ancient skeletons.

Two different types of rheumatic change were tentatively noted in the Lindow body during early investigations. In his preliminary examination of the severed foot, Robert Connolly suspected that the joint between the lower leg (tibia) and upper ankle bone (talus) showed osteo-arthritis, a condition not uncommon (especially in the spine) after the mid-thirties. However, more detailed study was later undertaken by the Rheumatology Unit of the Bristol University Medical School, who found no convincing evidence of the condition.

On the other hand, as already described, the CT scan displayed clear changes in some of the vertebral bodies in the lower back in the form of small 'herniations', or depressions into the main bodies of the vertebrae, called Schmorl's nodes. These are thought to be 'pressure erosions' caused by the intrusion of non-osseous intervertebral discs into the flat surfaces between the large spinal joints. These impressions may mimic early tuberculous abscesses, but in the case of the Lindow spine it was possible to remove segments (individual vertebrae) and look carefully at the surfaces of the vertebral bodies. These confirmed a diagnosis of Schmorl's nodes rather than a more destructive inflammation of the bones. Medically, these abnormalities are regarded as common and sub-clinical, producing no painful symptoms and thus requiring no treatment. From a biological point of view, however, they are interesting indications of biomechanical problems involving the spine. It is perhaps significant that these nodes tend to be found in the lower back, an area of the human body which has undergone considerable remodelling during its evolution to an erect posture. As a result of adapting to an upright stance, the curvature of the lower part of the spinal column has increased, and there seems little doubt that consequent stresses and strains are 'recorded' in the vertebrae, especially as so many demands are placed on the hands, arms and trunk (pulling, lifting, twisting, and so on).

This is by no means the only evidence of 'rheumatism' in earlier peoples. During the First World War, Sir Marc Ruffer was studying and writing on joint disease in the ancient Egyptians and in fact claimed that a serious progressive form of joint disease, ankylosing spondylitis of the spine ('bamboo spine'), was present. However, more recent studies, including research by the Bristol medical group who were consulted on the spinal changes in Lindow Man, raise doubts as to whether this condition was common at that period.

There was similar confusion over the diagnosis of changes in the vertebrae of Grauballe Man. Professor Glob describes the condition as 'incipient rheumatoid arthritis', but the radiological report mentions the formation of osteophytes (bone lipping) on the vertebrae at the back of the chest. These are very different rheumatic conditions, the latter being quite common in ancient skeletons of individuals of 35+ years, while the former is surprisingly rare in ancient peoples.

The Evidence for Worms

Even today, in the advanced societies of the world, several varieties of worm quite commonly enter the human body and establish themselves as parasites. Some are obvious to the naked eye when they are passed in the faeces, but others can be missed without a careful search for their minute eggs. Threadworms, roundworms, hookworms and tapeworms are the main groups likely to be present. The most destructive of these are the hookworms, which can cause chronic intestinal bleeding and anaemia, and the tapeworms, which can grow very large in the gut and encyst in the tissues of various parts of the body, including the brain.

Even in the earliest stages of examining the food remains in the tissues of Lindow Man, the eggs of two worms became clearly visible. One of these was the whipworm, *Trichuris trichiura*. (Its first name in fact means 'thread tail'.) Normally, its eggs are passed out of the body, but very large numbers will always remain present in parts of the gut at any one time. Worm eggs vary considerably from species to species

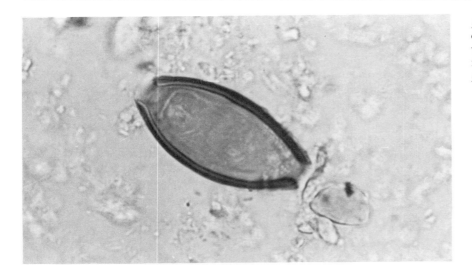

58 High-magnification view of an egg of the intestinal worm *Trichuris trichiura* from Lindow Man (length 51 microns).

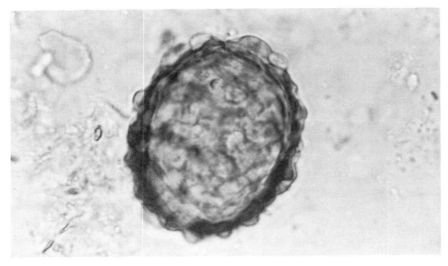

59 An egg (fertilised) of the worm *Ascaris lumbricoides* from Lindow Man (length 62 microns).

in size, shape and surface appearance. Those of *Trichuris* are roughly barrel-shaped, with polar plugs, and measure approximately 22 by 50 microns. They favour shade and moisture, and when the eggs are accidentally taken in from the ground or contaminated surfaces they grow to worms within a few weeks. A person who is heavily infested will experience a noticeable reduction in health, with poor appetite, feelings of weakness, diarrhoea, anaemia, weight loss and even some mild intestinal bleeding. These symptoms appear when some hundreds of worms are present, when the egg count can be over 30,000 per cubic centimetre.

The other worm eggs noted in Lindow Man were those of *Ascaris lumbricoides*, the maw worm, which may have become a greater health threat to humans as a result of the domestication of the pig. This is a large worm which can be 25 to 30 centimetres in length and up to 6 millimetres in diameter in the female, and a little smaller in the male. It fastens mainly onto the small intestine, where it feeds and lays an enormous number of eggs, perhaps as many as 200,000 a day! Under the microscope only the irregular exterior coat of the egg (roughly 65 by 45 microns) can be seen. To complicate identification, fertilised and unfertilised eggs are not identical in appearance. While *Ascaris* can produce lung disease, it more commonly causes problems in the intestines, from simple discomfort to more acute pain, diarrhoea and even nausea. Very occasionally the worms may cause intestinal blockages.

These, then, were the two worms certainly living in Lindow Man, although not, as far as can be ascertained, causing him much inconvenience. Because so little is known about the archaeology of these parasites, it was decided to investigate them in detail, and it is a reflection of the growth in this area of scientific research that a specialist, Andrew Jones, was available to make a detailed study of a sample of the eggs. Jones was able not only to confirm the presence of the two parasite species but, in the case of *Ascaris*, to show that there were both fertilised and unfertilised ova. He also concluded that, in comparison with specimens found in decayed faecal material from York and Oslo, the ova were generally in very good condition.

Eggs of this kind can be counted quite easily, and slides were therefore prepared and scanned at × 120 magnification. The results showed that *Trichuris* ova were present at a density of 3,500–5,700 eggs per gram of sample, while *Ascaris* gave counts of between 2,700 and 3,900 per gram. Moreover, it was possible to demonstrate that the mean dimensions of *Trichuris* eggs (length 55·0 microns and width 26·1 microns) were very similar to those of the modern human whipworm. The pig whipworm, which can also attack man, has eggs which are in fact considerably larger than those found in Lindow Man's intestine, and the same can be said of the eggs of whipworms from mice, rats, dogs, cattle and sheep. The varieties of *Ascaris* are more difficult to differentiate, however, and the eggs of the pig ascarid are identical in morphology and size to those of the human ascarid, although context argues for the human form, *A. lumbricoides*, being that present in the bog body. It is of course difficult from small samples and such waterlogged remains to be sure of the total worm burden of Lindow Man, although Jones tentatively suggests that his findings point to a relatively high infestation.

75

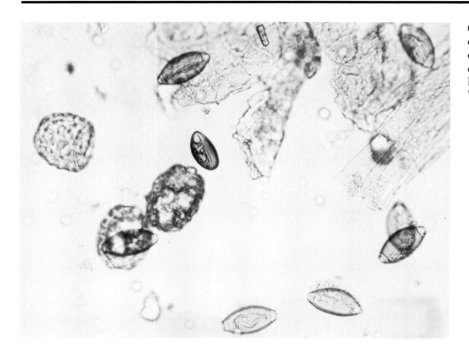

60 An assemblage of different types of intestinal worm egg, together with food debris, from a medieval latrine deposit at Winchester.

This is by no means the first archaeological evidence of these two worm species. The peat-bog people known as Karwinden Man, Grauballe Man, Tollund Man and the Drobnitz Girl all contained one or both. But examples have also been forthcoming from material as diverse as a Peruvian Inca child from a tomb in the Andes and faeces from medieval woodlined pits in Winchester and urban deposits in York. The European findings in particular seem to suggest that these parasites may have been far more of a health problem between about Iron Age and Saxon times than in the last few centuries.

5. Recreating an Environment

T he world of plants may seem remote from the investigation of an ancient human body, except of course for a consideration of the foods which may have been eaten. But a study of non-food plants, and their association in communities adapted to particular environments, can in fact provide us with much information relevant to a full evaluation of the circumstances of an individual's life and death.

Excluding the plant foods, which will be dealt with separately, plant remains can be considered at two levels, the macroscopic, concerned with larger debris, and the microscopic, primarily concerned with pollen. At an ordinary archaeological site, plant evidence is likely to be of various kinds, depending on whether the climate is temperate, arid or particularly cold. There may be charcoal from accidental or intentional wood fires, and carbonised grain or other food plant debris. Coprolites (dried faeces) may also be found, and in temperate climates these may simply take the form of partly decayed residues from man or domestic livestock. Flooring of plant origin and thatch may remain in collapsed or buried housing debris; and timbers from buildings or other constructions may be buried and preserved, especially if waterlogged. Beyond the actual area of habitation, additional plant information (in the form of pollen or larger debris) may be trapped and preserved in buried soils, peat bogs, lake and other deposits.

Because peat deposits consist mainly of compacted plant debris which has accumulated over many hundreds or even thousands of years, they are clearly a rich source of potential information about the distribution of plants, particularly in the immediate vicinity but also, to a lesser extent, over a wider area.

To most of us, bogs are bogs, but botanically they can be subdivided according to the way they have developed. In all cases we are dealing with acid wetland areas which encourage a characteristic vegetation. Valley bottoms and poorly drained hollows give rise to 'basin peats'. Shallowly domed 'raised bogs' and the usually larger, flat mantles of peat called 'blanket bogs' are ombrogenous; that is, they extend above the water level and need rain. In northern Britain, bogs such as the Lindow peatland are referred to as 'mosses', derived from Old English and Scandinavian words meaning peat-bogs.

The importance of such bogs lies in the fact that the wet, acidic and anaerobic conditions inhibit decay, with a consequent build-up of vegetable remains. The surface of the bog may not only change in terms of its topographic height (and the depth of peat formed) but will inevitably show some vegetational transformations. There may be pools of open water, perhaps especially after the winter saturation of the peat, and there will be hummocks consisting of such plants as bog moss (*Sphagnum* spp.), ling (*Calluna vulgaris*), cotton-grass (*Eriophorum vaginatum*), cranberry (*Vaccinium oxycoccos*) and others (Plate II). Each species tends to have its own special niche within the bog, related partly to the water level. Peat cover may be relatively thin or up to several metres thick. When it is over two or three feet in depth, it can be dug out for fuel or other purposes, the living upper layer being skinned off and back-stacked into the bog. Before machine-cutting took over, peats were cut into brick shapes and stacked to mature. The antiquity of such fuel cutting goes back into prehistory, and there is evidence that some of the Danish bog bodies were placed into old peat cuttings.

The question arose as to whether Lindow Man was buried deep into the bog or whether he was left on the surface, perhaps submerged in a pool, and was gradually covered by rapidly forming peat. The latter interpretation is indicated by most of the evidence provided by plant debris, pollen and the remains of insects and other invertebrates.

The macrofossils, or large pieces of plant debris, in the Lindow Moss were studied in detail by Keith Barber of Southampton University, using so-called monoliths (vertical columns) cut through a depth of peat near the body. Although *Sphagnum* was abundant, the varieties present were *S. imbricatum*, a species which is now becoming quite rare, and two others. A close study of the *Sphagnum* species and associated algae suggests that there may have been some shallow pool formation at about the time of the death of Lindow Man. The samples also provided evidence of gradual infilling of the pool, and Dr Barber sees this as rapidly covering Lindow Man's body within a few years. With further vegetational growth and change, and somewhat drier surface conditions encouraging the increase in cotton-grass and *Sphagna acutifolia*, the body would have been well covered and secured against further microbial attack.

61 The microscopic appearance of pollen grains, showing the variation in shape and size which occurs between different species.

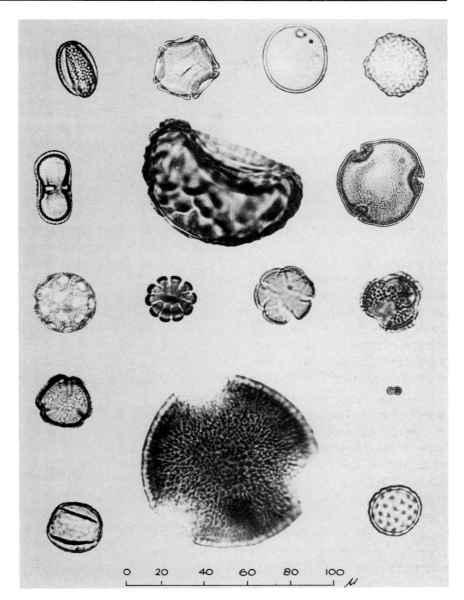

Pollen, Plants and Prehistory

Although perhaps best known for the 'hay fever' and other seasonal allergies it can produce, pollen has become an extremely important factor in some aspects of archaeological interpretation. Pollen grains, the microstructures which enable flowering plants to be fertilised, are released into the surrounding environment and may be carried some distance by air currents. However, the majority will fall locally, so that frequencies of pollen grains can be a guide to the relative frequencies of plants in a particular area. The considerable changes in vegetation which have occurred in Europe since glacial times can be demonstrated by reference to pollen frequencies, and this method has proved a useful adjunct to the dating of archaeological remains. Pollen analysis has also been increasingly used to evaluate changes in vegetation linked to human activity over the past few thousand years. In particular, the ratio of tree pollen to non-tree pollen (such as light-demanding herbs and cereals) may provide important information about the extent to which human communities have reduced woodland or cultivated the land.

While many different types of deposit may encourage the preservation of pollen grains, peat is a particularly rich source of these microstructures, for the original acid waterlogged bogs provided ideal anaerobic environments for the grains to rest in. Depending on the quality of preservation, the pollen grains usually retain their shape, which varies according to their species. This enables pollen to be identified in the laboratory, usually to genus and sometimes to species level. It is no wonder, then, that pollen from peat deposits surrounding human remains has been studied for the information it can provide about the environment, although this has not perhaps been as common as one might have hoped.

The care with which pollen data must be evaluated is well illustrated by the study made of the peat deposits associated with Grauballe Man. He was discovered towards the top of a small peat bog called Nebelgaard Mose which, at its deepest point, had originally extended 8 metres in depth. Through this depth the pollen 'picture' changed, and contrasting zones could be distinguished. The Grauballe body rested in layer 5, an upper *Sphagnum* peat, which was found to contain the pollen. Because this cereal is known to have arrived in Denmark no earlier than Roman Iron Age times, the presence of its pollen in association with the body provided useful dating evidence. Secondly, an interesting feature of these strips of upper *Sphagnum* peat was that they lay at varying depths from the surface, suggesting that this particular peat was forming on earlier peat cuttings. In the writings of Pliny the Elder (AD 23–79) we learn that peat was being used as fuel in northern Germany, and peat cutting in the Iron Age has been demonstrated archaeologically in Jutland, so this interpretation of the site where Grauballe Man was buried is not unreasonable. In all, six separate samples of peat were taken from around his body, and in one specimen from just below it, the rye pollen is clearly present. This indicates without much doubt that the body was not placed on a well-cut surface of old peat, but rather on a surface on which new peat moss was growing. A final conclusion that can be drawn from the pollen is that the surrounding area was being extensively cultivated at that time and that much of the local woodland had been cleared to give way to large commons, pasture lands and fields of barley and rye.

To what extent can similar interpretations be made from the Lindow Moss pollen evidence? This aspect was in the hands of Frank Oldfield and colleagues, and their findings again show the different strands of information that can be derived from the close study of the peat and pollen. On the discovery of the body and its subsequent excavation, an important first task was to analyse the relationship of the corpse to the vegetation surrounding it. Peat samples were therefore taken vertically through the peat alongside the body, and further samples were collected from various points on the body itself. The peat around it was by no means homogeneous. A major feature was evidence of an extensive fresh-water pool, which may perhaps have existed for quite a few years, and part of the body (upper arms and torso) seem to have been resting in the pool mud. In the head region was a hummock of somewhat different peat containing much heather (*Calluna vulgaris*) and cotton-grass (*Eriophorum vaginatum*), probably situated at the water's edge. The forearms were resting in a slightly different *Eriophorum* peat, which could have provided less anaerobic conditions at times, thus allowing localised decomposition of the lower arms and hands. Subtle vegetational changes then took place, including the development of peat containing much bog moss (*Sphagnum* spp.) and cranberry (*Vaccinium oxycoccos*), so that the pool slowly filled in and the body became fully 'sealed off'. About 2·5 metres of peat eventually covered it.

When Professor Oldfield and his colleagues came to evaluate the pollen frequencies in these successive deposits, a number of important facts emerged. In the sampled vertical sections through the peat, there is no evidence of human activity below 61 centimetres. At about 60 centimetres some changes can be detected, with a decline in oak pollen and an increase in birch, alder, grasses and bracken. These changes may have been the result of local human settlements or perhaps just a response to minor climatic changes. Over the next few centimetres, to 50 centimetres, there is clear evidence of the impact of man in the area, with the pollen of cereals and land-clearance weeds such as docks, plantain and mugwort. Beyond this, higher in the peat, human activity has had a noticeable impact on the local vegetation, with a very marked decline in pine and oak.

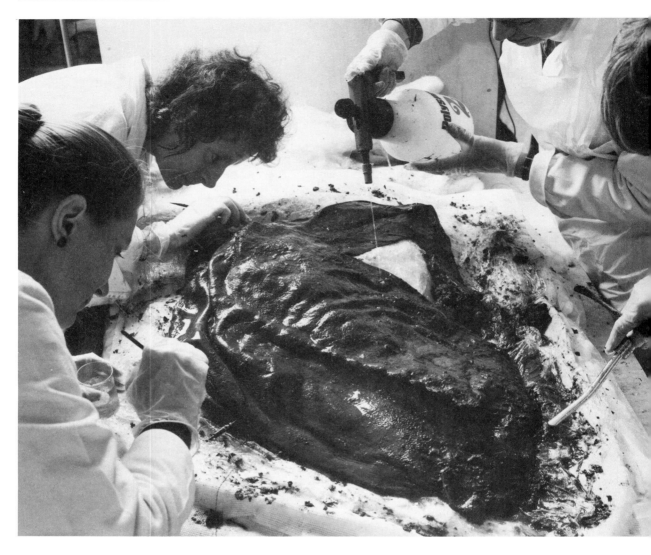

The body was therefore positioned within a sequence of vegetational change, its situation corresponding to the beginnings of a major forest clearance and increased farming activity. Pollen is in evidence from cereals such as wheat and/or barley and oats, although probably not rye. It thus seems possible to conclude that Lindow Man was left partly immersed in a muddy pool at a time when considerable changes were taking place in the surrounding countryside. The slight differences in vegetation, and the relationship of the body to them, probably explain the uneven preservation of different parts of the corpse.

62 Cleaning the back of Lindow Man. Distilled water is being sprayed on to keep the skin moist. Maureen Girling (top left) looks carefully for insect debris close to the body surface.

Invertebrates

Indicators of the environment surrounding an ancient burial can be of many kinds, and studies will take into account not only the species likely to be found in a particular habitat but also exactly what is likely to be preserved in particular burial conditions. Thus, in acid peat, the calcareous shells of molluscs are likely to decay, while the exoskeletons of insects and some other invertebrates are made of a sufficiently tough material to survive. Studies of insects are now becoming a more common feature of bioarchaeological research. In particular, Coleoptera (beetle) remains, which are found at numerous sites, even in northern Europe, can sometimes provide significant environmental information. This had hitherto been a neglected area in bog body studies, so the Lindow project was lucky to have the support of a number of 'archaeo-entomologists', the general study being in the hands of the late Maureen Girling.

Ten samples were investigated, in the form both of peat and of 'washings' from the body surface. Thus, head and beard and hair, the ear region, abdomen, spine and back were all checked. Compared with some archaeological samples, only modest numbers of insect remains were found, and these were mainly fragmentary, representing only certain parts of the external skeleton (such as wingcases, heads, etc.). This made classification difficult, but nevertheless thirty-five separate taxonomic categories of insect were identified (nearly half of these to species level). In terms of major groups of invertebrates, five insect families were identified, as well as two spiders and some mites.

Beetles (*Coleoptera*)

Most of the beetle evidence reflected the nature of the bog environment and was not influenced by the corpse in the vicinity. Dr Girling concluded that the presence of these Coleoptera supported the picture of neutral to acid bog conditions, 'with peaty pools fringed with wetland plants and other bog vegetation growing in the vicinity'. Taking as an example the occurrence of a reddish-coloured water beetle, *Hydroporus obscurus*, records from the north indicate that it is associated with acid waters such as *Sphagnum* pools, a fact which corroborates the plant evidence. The presence of fragments of the family Scirtidae similarly suggests peaty pools.

Other species, including plant-feeding beetles, indicate or confirm the nature of some of the vegetation surrounding the pools. For instance, *Plateumaris discolor* feeds on cotton-grass, and *Chaetocnema sahlbergi* might have been living on cranberry. The presence of the weevils *Rhynchaenus* and *Rhyncolus lignarius* suggests that there were at least some trees in the vicinity.

It may well be especially significant that the carrion-feeding beetle *Paralister* was present, as it could have been attracted by the corpse. Admittedly, only one example was found – on the back of Lindow Man – but others may have been excluded from the samples.

Flies (*Diptera*)

A small number of the insect remains were handed on to P. Skidmore of Doncaster Museum and Art Gallery. His specialist note on certain Diptera (true flies) was significant by the relative lack of fly evidence. Even allowing for the fact that some kinds of fly would not be about in the winter, there was nevertheless an impressive absence of a 'necrophilous fauna' of the kind which could certainly be expected if the corpse had been exposed to the atmosphere for a while, rather than submerged in the bog.

'Bloodworms' (*Chironomidae*)

Within the large insect group Diptera there is a family of small two-winged gnat-like flies (or non-biting midges) rather similar to mosquitoes. These have an aquatic larval stage which, in some species, can display distinctive colours. Their name 'bloodworm' is derived from the fact that some larvae of this group have the red pigment haemoglobin in the blood, and thus seem to be better able to breathe in stagnant water containing little oxygen. The larvae all resemble one another, being slender and segmented, with a clearly demarcated head. At the back, on the underside of the eleventh segment of the body, are the so-called 'blood gills', the blood-filled tubes thought to be important in oxygen exchange. Although the larvae of various species look relatively similar, their ways of life differ considerably. Some live in mud; others in calcium deposits produced by algae from hard water; yet others construct long galleries in aquatic plants. Although 2,000 species are known, only about 400 occur in Britain, and only two or three are known to exist in the Lindow bog environment.

Not all parts of the larva survive in the peat deposit, but the tough head capsule is especially likely to resist decay. Fragments can be picked out while the remains of Coleoptera are being sorted under the binocular microscope. However, it is one thing to recognise chironomid pieces, but quite another to identify to a genus or species level. Judith Dayton was able to show that the larvae belonged to the sub-family Orthocladiinae, a group found mainly in cold and temperate zones. One genus which seemed likely in the Lindow peat was *Smittia*, but other forms could not be named with certainty. The presence of *Smittia*, however, probably indicates boggy rather than normally open-water conditions, with plenty of vegetation for the herbivorous species of Orthocladiinae to feed on.

Waterfleas (*Cladocera*)

These small, usually microscopic, crustaceans are very common and their remains can be picked out and identified from lake and bog deposits. Recently, they have proved increasingly useful in the reconstruction of ancient environments. Most waterfleas live in stagnant fresh water, but a few are marine, and most of us are acquainted with them only as aquarium fish food. Called fleas because of their jerky method of locomotion, they are in fact a very different creature from the human flea. As Fig. 63 shows, waterfleas are generally globular in overall shape, although there is considerable variation in the 400 or so species which have been described (over 80 of which are endemic to Europe). The head has a 'cephalic shield' with complex antennae. The body is not greatly segmented, and there are up to six pairs of legs.

The eggs of waterfleas can be transported by water birds and other animals and so fairly rapidly introduced into new environments, including the relatively rare micro-environment surrounding a dead human body! From an evolutionary point of view, the cladocerans have not changed for many thousands of years, and it can thus safely be assumed that their ecology has also remained the same over this long period. Although under the microscope the bodies of waterfleas look extremely fragile, certain parts of them may be found in abundance in peat deposits, especially the large outer body shell (carapace), the head shield and the so-called post-abdomen (a hind section).

Identification of fragments is by no means easy, but Judith Dayton, who undertook this specialist work, was able to distinguish five species. The commonest of these appeared to be a species of *Alona* and many examples were tuberculated, a characteristic thought to be indicative of a boggy environment. Furthermore, the occurrence of so-called resting eggs, probably also of *Alona*, is interpreted as suggesting that conditions were unsuitable for these waterfleas, which prefer open water. *Alonella* was also well in evidence, as were the head shields and carapaces of *Pseudochydorus globosus*. The limited number of species present further supports the view that the environment was not ideal and therefore probably boggy. And it is perhaps significant

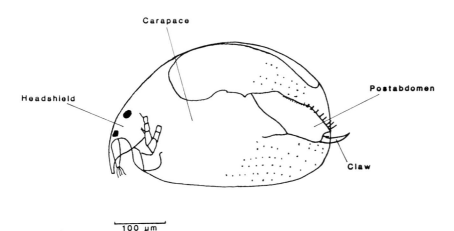

64 (*below left*) Fragment of what appears to be the same species, collected from the peat immediately surrounding Lindow Man.

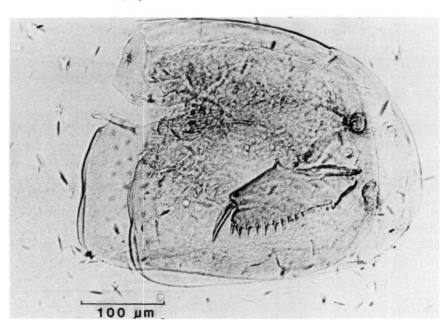

65-67 (*opposite*) Other kinds of invertebrate evidence associated with ancient human remains: (*top*) large numbers of fly puparia in the wrappings from Egyptian mummy 1770; (*bottom left*) almost complete, naturally dried head louse (*Pediculus humanus*) from a pre-Columbian body excavated at Ancon, Peru; (*bottom right*) section through tissues of an Egyptian eye, showing an intrusive larva, probably of a *Piophila* fly. This could have caused an eye disease in life (ocular myiasis), but might have entered *post mortem* ($\times$ 300).

that *Alona rustica*, which was common in the peat, is often associated with small acid pools. This interpretation would seem to fit in with the plant evidence as well.

Perhaps the most intriguing fact is the presence of *Pseudochydorus globosus*, which is a scavenger. Its diet usually consists of the carcasses of other crustaceans, and it is therefore worth noting that these were in plentiful supply around the body of Lindow Man. Again, such evidence argues for the corpse having initially been exposed on the surface of the bog rather than buried deep into the existing peat.

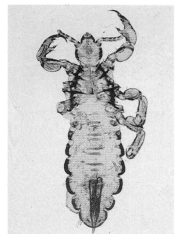

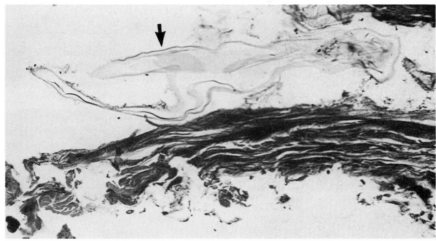

The Case of the Moving Fingernails

Some months after the initial work on the Lindow body, when the photographs were being examined for possible publication, the significance of one fact suddenly emerged. Perhaps as a result of lighting and photographic contrasts, it became clearer that several of the nails were some distance away from the end finger bones. Like those of Tollund Man, the forearms and fingers showed noticeable decomposition, but in Lindow Man something had also caused considerable lateral displacement of the nails within the peat. Had the

87

body or the arms moved, as a result perhaps of settling into the soft upper surface peat, and after some degree of decomposition? Or, if the body had initially been submerged in a peaty pool while this restricted decomposition took place, could the nails have floated off when minor currents or plant growth caused some movement or disturbance in the water? Not all the nails were in fact accounted for in the peat block brought back to the laboratory with the body. This suggests that other nails had drifted into the area just beyond the hands, which had been trimmed away by the peat-cutting machine. The extent of the disturbance and shunting of the nails in the peat will never be known. However, what evidence there is, argues against the interment of the body in deeper levels of peat, as the more compact, older peat would not have allowed the nails to become detached and to move in this way.

The local environmental picture developing from all this evidence, then, is that of a bog in which acid pools may periodically have formed, into one of which the body of Lindow Man was perhaps deposited.

68 Close-up of three of Lindow Man's fingernails, dispersed in the region of the decayed forearm.

Plate II A blanket bog in North Wales, with pools, cotton-grass and pale green bog moss (*Sphagnum*).

Plate III Woollen clothing found on peat bodies from (left to right) Barrock in Caithness, Arnish Moor in Lewis and Gunnister in Shetland (Edinburgh, Royal Museum of Scotland).

Plate I (*previous page*) Lindow Man emerges from the peat.

Plate IV Detail of the elaborate tattoo, indicative of a high social status in life, on the right arm of a Scythian chieftain from barrow 2 at Pazyryk (Leningrad, State Hermitage Museum).

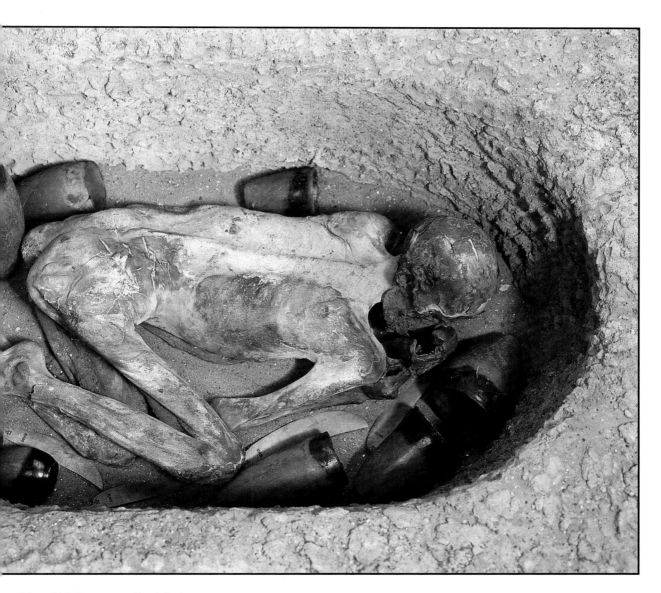

Plate V The naturally dried predynastic Egyptian body known as 'Ginger', found in a shallow grave at Gebelein and dating from about 3200 BC (British Museum).

Plate VI Well-preserved early
Peruvian mummy, displaying a
beautiful feather headdress
(London, Museum of Mankind).

Plate VII The body of a medieval
six-month-old Eskimo boy, from
Qilakitsok, Greenland (Greenland
Museum)

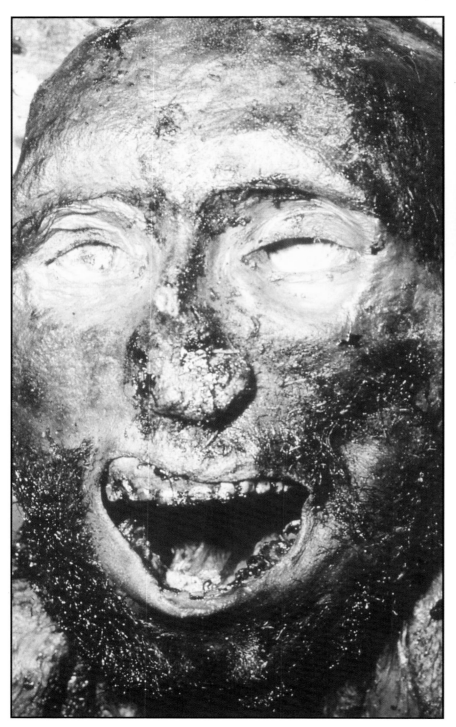

Plate VIII The face of the medieval St Bees man. The eyes were especially well preserved.

Plate IX Incision into the chest of the St Bees man, showing the blood still red.

6. The Last Meal

Archaeologists have long been interested in the food eaten by former peoples. Diet has changed radically in the course of human cultural evolution, from palaeolithic hunting and collecting to varying types of farming. Our own 'advanced' societies are probably distinguished by food abuse, over-eating and unbalanced diets, but these problems extend back over millennia. Careful scientific work on food debris associated with human habitations developed during the first half of the nineteenth century. By 1866 the botanist Professor Oswald Heer had produced a substantial work on the *Plants of the Lake Dwellings*, a study of well-preserved food remains from Swiss lake sites.

Sadly, it is also in the nineteenth century that we find the first evidence of crooked dealings in bioarchaeology. Alphonse de Candolle, in his classic work on the *Origin of Cultivated Plants* (1882) wrote: 'The fruits, seeds and different portions of plants taken from ancient Egyptian tombs, and the drawings which surround them in the pyramids, have given rise to most important researches, which I shall often have to mention. Nevertheless, there is a possible source of error; the fraudulent introduction of modern plants into the sarcophagi of the mummies. This was easily discovered in the case of some grains of maize, for instance, a plant of American origin, which were introduced by the Arabs; but species cultivated in Egypt within the last two or three thousand years may have been added, which would thus appear to have belonged to an earlier period.'

There is now much well-stratified, usually carbonised, evidence of plant food and bone debris, which enables us reliably to reconstruct the nature of foods used in the past. However, there is always particular interest in the remains of individual meals, represented either by food residue preserved in the alimentary canal of bodies or skeletons, or by faeces deposited and preserved in latrines or elsewhere. In this respect, new levels of detailed investigation were achieved by the phyto-archaeologist Hans Helbaek with the discovery after the Second World War of Danish bog bodies in which stomach

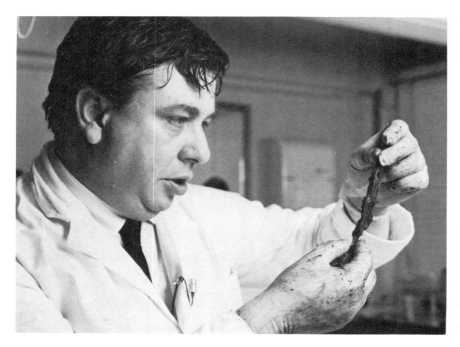

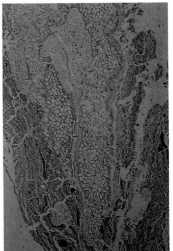

69 James Bourke, the surgeon, removes the remains of Lindow Man's intestinal tract.

70 Photomicrograph of the upper small intestine of Lindow Man, showing preservation of collagen tissue but the loss of specialised mucosal or lining cells.

remains had been preserved. There was also a large quantity of food residue (610 cubic centimetres) in Grauballe Man (compared with 275 cubic centimetres in the Tollund stomach). The remains looked like a 'fine-grained brown mud', as in Lindow Man, but contained far more seed fragments, as well as some small pieces of bone and, rather oddly, a 'couple of pebbles'! The total Grauballe sample added up to millions of particles, but Helbaek concentrated on the larger ones. In view of the comparatively large pieces of plant food, the bone fragments (up to 7 millimetres long) and even the pebbles, Helbaek postulates that the food was eaten (perhaps one should say gulped down) in the form of a predominantly cereal gruel, with some meat and other stored plant food but without seasonal vegetables, fruits or berries. This was used to support his theory that the man's death occurred in the winter and may have been part of the 'sanguinary rites of the Iron Age Midwinter Festival'.

Detailed work on Lindow Man's food residue (about 20 grams in all) was carried out by Tim Holden, with the collaboration of Gordon Hillman and other specialists. Sub-samples were taken for thorough microscopic identification – no easy task in the case of such well-chewed ancient evidence! Nevertheless, Table 3 shows that probably more than a dozen varieties of plant were represented, and of these, cereals were by far the most common. In fact, these were often found

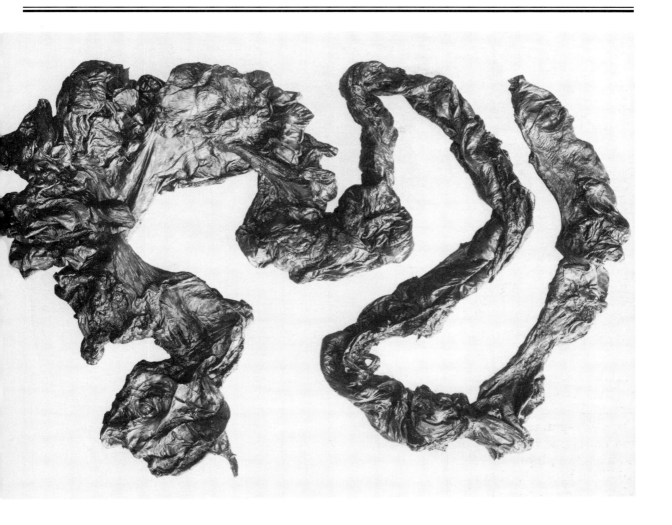

71 **Part of the preserved gut of Tollund Man.**

in the form of the inner layers of bran (perisperm and spermoderm) which had surrounded the starchy main part of the cereal. The cellular detail and contrasts in these layers made it possible to attempt identification down to species level. The modern equivalent would be identifying the cereals used in wholemeal bread after most of the starchy nutritious component had been taken out. Basic cereal anatomy is given in Figs 72-74, and it should be noted that in addition to the bran layers, chaff, rachis internodes and glume bases were also found. From the careful evaluation of these minute layers of cell coats surrounding the starchy cereal grains, it was possible to demonstrate the probable presence of emmer and spelt wheats, as well as barley and oats (although this last cereal could have been a wild variety).

Table 3
Identified material in the stomach and intestine of Lindow Man

Species	Identified Components	Quantity
Sphagnum spp.	leaves and stems	xx
Chenopodium album	seed fragments	x
Chenopodium/Atriplex type	small seed fragments	x
Umbelliferae indet.	seed fragment	x
Polygonum lapathifolium $	seed fragment	x
Polygonum convolvulus	seed fragment	x
Calluna vulgaris	leaf	x
Rumex sp.	small seed fragments	x
Galeopsis type	seed fragments	x
Bromus sp.	bran fragments	xxx
Wheat:		
Triticum dicoccum $	glume bases	x
Triticum spelta $	glume bases	x
Triticum indet. $	glume bases	xx
Wheat/rye:		
Triticum/secale indet.	bran fragments	xxxx
Barley:		
Hordeum sp. $	glumes, paleas, rachillas, lemmas	xxx
Hordeum sp.	bran fragments	xx
Oats:		
Avena sp.	bran fragments	xx
Oats/barley:		
Avena/Hordeum indet.	bran fragments	x
Cereal indet.	glume, paleas, lemma fragments	xxxx
Carbonised fragments		x
Fungi	hyphae, spores	x
Small animal hairs		xx
Fine sand		x

x = less than 5 items; xx = between 6 and 19 items; xxx = 20-99 items;
xxxx = 100 + items. $ = identifications by Gordon Hillman.

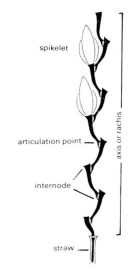

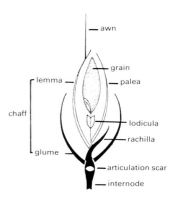

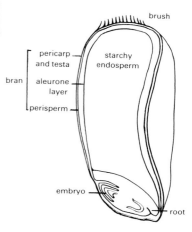

In comparison with the domestic cereals, other possible foods (or accidental inclusions with food) formed only a small part of the residue. There were relatively numerous fragments of brome grass, but few seeds or other plants. Of these, *Sphagnum, Chenopodium, Polygonum, Calluna, Rumex* and *Galeopsis* were probably present in small amounts, and in most cases may have been accidental inclusions. Minute fragments of carbonised food debris may suggest that slightly charred bread had been eaten, and indeed the application of a new technique, electron spin resonance, to the evaluation of cooking temperatures suggests that bread was a major food item. Many animal

72-74 (*left*) The basic anatomy of cereal plants and a wheat grain (after Helbaek and others).

75, 76 Variation in the microscopic anatomy of cereal fragments from the gut of Lindow Man: (*top*) cell structure of barley chaff; (*bottom*) cell (testa) layers, probably of wheat, showing a chequerboard pattern.

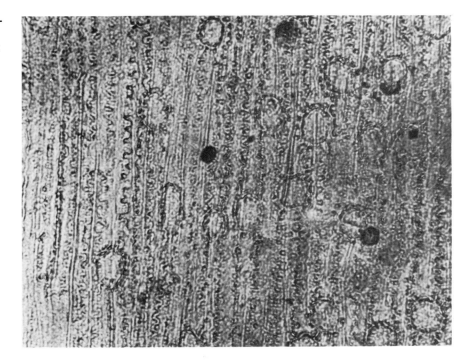

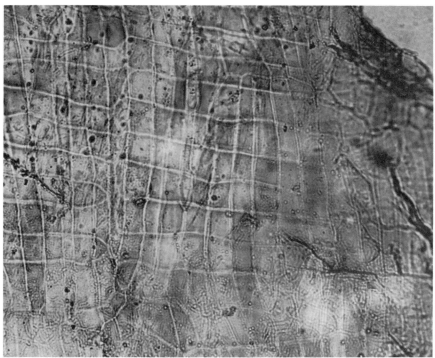

hairs were also found. Identification of these proved difficult, owing to the absence of the more diagnostic guard hairs, but they seem likely to have come from smaller mammals and either to have been swallowed with meat or to have been contaminating the cereals, and are therefore possible indications of crop storage pests.

It is also worth mentioning that fungal hyphae and spores were found associated with some cereal fragments. Identification of these is still being undertaken, but the species probably include *Ustilago hordei*, a crop plant disease which Helbaek also found in the stomach of Grauballe Man.

So what can we say about the last meal of Lindow Man? He had far fewer remains in his alimentary tract than the Grauballe and Tollund individuals, and one should really perhaps refer to a 'snack' rather than a full-blown meal. Was this in the form of conventional prisoners' fare – 'bread and water' – or a gruel? The carbonised fragments might argue a little more strongly for a slightly charred bread, but of course the gruel pot could have scorched! The probable absence of rye is not surprising, as it was not a common cereal in prehistoric Britain. Compared with the food residue studied in Danish bodies, relatively few species are represented in Lindow Man, and a number of these are very likely to be accidental. The plant food debris in Lindow Man also seems to be finer in terms of fragment size. Moreover, while the Grauballe 'muesli' contained over sixty plant species, and the Borre Fen man made do on non-cereal wild and weed species, there seems to be nothing special about Lindow Man's repast except its simplicity. It was also high in fibre, so he would not have suffered from constipation or diverticulitis.

Pollen from the Gut

It may seem unimportant to consider the pollen mixed with the food residue when there is so much more pollen available for study in the peat immediately surrounding the body. However, there are four good reasons for undertaking this additional research. First, while the pollen in the peat next to the body had collected over many months or years, there was a chance that pollen breathed in or resting on the food might give a clue to the season of death. Secondly, any pollen swallowed with the food might help to establish the nature of the food eaten; and, thirdly, there was even a chance of finding pollen which was foreign to the region (having been carried to the site, for instance, on the food). Finally, unexpected pollen might accidentally have been taken in with medicinal potions or ritual libations, or for other special reasons. While this may seem unlikely, it should be remembered that the stomach contents of Grauballe Man contained a wide range of plant species which some scholars see as evidence of a form of ritual 'last supper'.

Thus, while plants from the peat were being intensively studied in Liverpool and Southampton, Rob Scaife, a research palynologist in London, was investigating Lindow Man's gut. In all, he examined five sub-samples of the food residue from parts of the stomach and smaller intestine, and counted the identifiable pollen grains. The results showed that, in marked contrast to the peat samples from around the body, the gut pollen was predominantly derived from cereal plants. What did this mean? Had the man died in early summer, when the cornfields were giving off their pollen clouds? This might seem a satisfactory answer, but it is not easy to reach conclusions as to seasonality from such pollen, as it is known that it may lodge on the growing cereal inflorescences. These cereal structures would also act as 'traps' for other pollen, especially of arable weeds intimately associated with the cultivation of cereal crops. It is not surprising, then, that pollen of Cruciferae, *Chenopodium*, *Plantago* and other weed types were also identified in the sample.

Furthermore, Scaife found a similar combination of cereal and weed pollens in a stomach sample from Grauballe Man sent from Denmark, although in Lindow Man the cereal pollen was more predominant. In fact, the larger plant debris from Grauballe Man, already studied by Hans Helbaek, showed that a surprisingly large range of plant species was represented in the stomach, and not just as pollen. The obvious conclusion from this difference is that Lindow Man was eating 'cleaner' cereals, less contaminated with weed plants.

Pollen, Paganism and Poison: the Question of Mistletoe
Mistletoe has been associated with Christmas festivities in Britain for many decades, and is claimed by some to have associations extending back to rituals of millennia ago. The Druids, for example, about whom, admittedly, much that is highly dubious has been written, are said to have used mistletoe in their religious ceremonies. It is parasitic on a variety of deciduous trees and, far less commonly, on conifers. The berries are claimed to be poisonous, but there are records of their use in herbal remedies.

Tantalising, though limited, evidence of this plant was found in Lindow Man's gut in the form of pollen grains (no seeds from the berries were noted), and small numbers of these were found in the intestinal tract. Where did this mistletoe pollen come from? Had there been evidence of berries, the pollen might have been accidentally sticking to them. It could also have been accidentally incorporated into herbal remedies, but there was no evidence of any other part of the plant. One exciting possibility is that the pollen came from flowering plants and had been breathed into the mouth or brought in on food just before the death of Lindow Man. If that is the case, then we can fix the time of his death somewhere in March or April. This would certainly help to explain the preservation of the body, for after the winter months the water would still be cold, discouraging decay and allowing time for the 'juices' of the bog to help to preserve some of the tissues. Moreover, it lends weight to the theory that Lindow Man may have been a sacrificial victim, killed as part of a ritual, linked perhaps with rites of spring.

Anne Ross, who has much experience of Celtic traditions and folklore, views the mistletoe pollen as highly significant, especially in relation to the cut throat, the possible garrotting and the submergence of the Lindow body in the bog. She points out that even the name Lindow could have the ominous meaning of 'Black Pool' (*llyn* is lake in Welsh; *dow* could be an anglicised Welsh *du* or Gaelic *dubh*, meaning black).

The Romans record that sacrifices were made by Celtic tribes to their gods. Each god could demand a specific form of death, but there is also evidence of a 'trinity', a ritually significant combination of violent acts to despatch the individual to the next world. Such sacrifice could have ensured fertility in their womenfolk, land or livestock, or have been intended to please and appease the gods. It could be significant, in this respect, that the Druids of Roman times believed that mistletoe, taken in a drink, restored fecundity to barren animals.

Anne Ross also considers that the presence of slightly charred cereal in Lindow Man's stomach may have related and ritual significance, rather than just being evidence of careless cooking or baking. It seems a long jump from the examination of a bog body to Celtic cake ceremonies and the significance of blackened bread, but clearly every possible link needs to be considered. In the eighteenth century, an ancient custom was still recorded in Perthshire where at the 'Beltain festival' a special bannock was broken up and distributed amongst those present. The person unlucky enough to get a blackened portion was named the 'devoted' (i.e. to the gods for sacrifice) and was then referred to as 'dead'.

What at first sight may seem to be totally unassociated facts can thus be drawn together to give a very different interpretation. There is unlikely to be any more certain proof of the ritual aspects of Lindow Man's end, but a consideration of Celtic mythology and folklore certainly gives new meaning to some of the existing facts.

7. Beyond the Bog Body

The watery, anaerobic environment of the bog is not the only one which is conducive to the preservation of human remains other than the skeleton. Cold temperatures such as those occurring in Greenland or the underground tombs in Siberia, and the warm, dry climate of Egypt, Arizona or coastal Peru provide the two contrasting poles of environmental variation. But in between is a range of other micro-environments which have inhibited decay, and in some of these it is difficult to understand why preservation is in fact as good as it is. Indeed, there is a need for a great deal more scientific research into this whole question. In what follows, therefore, my concern will be limited to reviewing the kinds of sites which have encouraged particularly good preservation.

Northern European Bog Bodies

By far the most thorough exploration of written sources for records of bodies found in peat has been made by Dr Alfred Dieck. In view of the fact that he has been able to document 690 cases, the actual number of bog bodies which have been discovered must be well in excess of this. Indeed, as this book was being prepared, a new bog body was autopsied in Dublin and information became available on another one which has been left in the peat for reasons of principle.

In terms of distribution by countries, numbers are of course related to the occurrence of peat deposits and the extent to which they have been worked. Thus, based on Dieck's figures, Denmark, although a relatively small country, has produced at least 166 bog people, Germany 215, Holland 48, and Britain and Ireland at least 77. This last figure has now been revised by Briggs and Turner, who list no fewer than 120 sites. The dating of most of these remains spans from Iron Age and Roman times to the medieval and post-medieval periods. In some cases, little was left of the body, and sometimes the clothing was preserved better than the corpse. Many of the bodies were found some decades ago and are no longer available for study. Nowadays, since the introduction of peat-cutting machinery, the

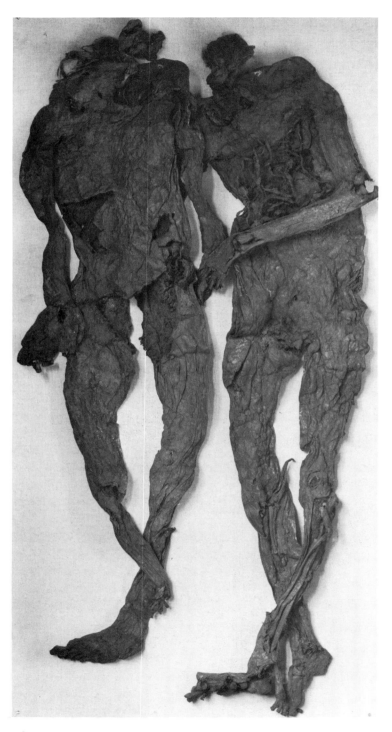

77 The 'Darby and Joan' of bog bodies, found in 1904 in a peat deposit at Werdingerveen, Holland. Note the man's arm extending behind the woman's back. The damage to the heads is probably the result of peat-cutting (Assen, Provincial Museum of Drenthe).

78 The Huldre Fen Woman, discovered over 100 years ago in Denmark. The arm may have been hacked off in life (Copenhagen, National Museum).

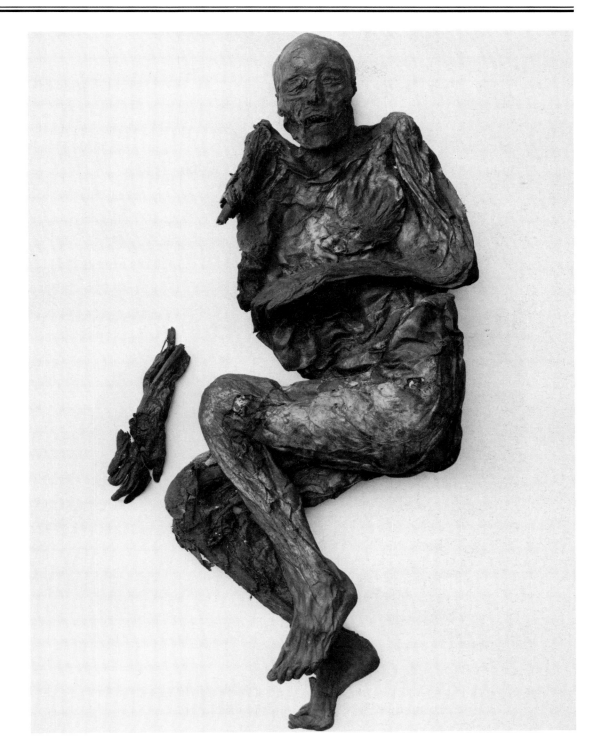

chances of finding bog bodies are reduced, although fortunately the scanning of the machine conveyor belt, as at the Lindow plant, ensures that some may still be picked up.

The great variation in the degree of preservation of these bodies is very puzzling indeed. The body of Grauballe Man, except for some squashing and flattening, was remarkably well preserved. Tissues as different as those of the brain, liver, lungs and testicles were all preserved, and even the fingerprints could be studied in detail. Tollund Man displayed an odd patchy decay to the arms and legs, even though the head and feet were beautifully preserved. Lindow Man shows a similar decay of the arms and most of the internal organs, although the rest of the external surface is relatively intact. At the other extreme, one should mention a body from Damendorf, north Germany, of which only extremely flattened skin, nails and hair remained.

Other European Finds

Except in the case of bog people, the soft tissues of bodies found in Europe have not normally been preserved. The one exception to this is hair, which is particularly resistant. Remains of hair have been found at various sites, and samples from the Roman site of Poundbury, Dorset, have recently been described and studied in detail.

The most complete body yet found in Europe is that of the medieval nobleman discovered at St Bees Priory, Cumbria, in 1981 (Plates VIII and IX). During excavations, Deirdre O'Sullivan and her colleagues came across two groups of burials. One was presumably the monks' cemetery, dating from about AD 1120–1300. The other was probably that of the secular population, and in this group was the preserved body. Within a well-constructed vault was a 'lead coffin', placed inside an iron-bound wooden coffin and packed with grey clay. In fact the 'lead coffin' was nothing more than a sheet of lead wrapped around the body. When the lead was opened up, a shrouded figure was revealed. The body was eventually unwrapped and studied in detail before being reburied. When the outer and inner shrouds and the waxy embalming material were removed, a remarkably well-preserved body appeared to view, naked but for two pieces of string around the neck and penis (part of the 'laying out' practice of the day). We find stories of the miraculous preservation of ancient dignitaries and some accounts of preserved bodies of medieval or post-medieval date, but the St Bees man provides first-hand evidence of a body in an exceptional state of preservation. Dr Eddie Tapp, who undertook the autopsy, was careful to note how the body looked when first

79 The bog woman recently discovered at Meenybradan, Ireland, before the autopsy investigation carried out by Dr Jack Harbison (Dublin, Irish National Museum).

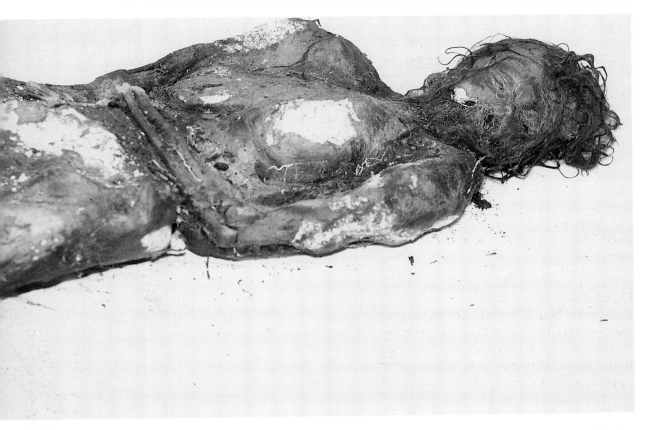

80 The St Bees body *in situ*, wrapped in a lead sheet and lying next to an ordinary human skeleton.

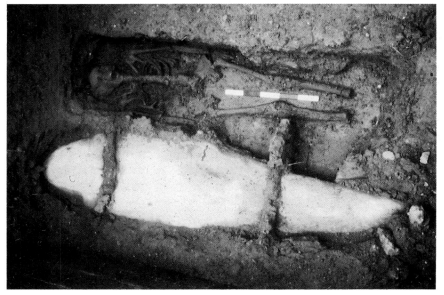

unwrapped. The skin had a fresh pink appearance, which quickly faded. The eyes were in good condition, and the mucosa of the mouth looked fresh at first. Internal tissues were similarly well preserved, indeed the blood vessels even appeared to contain 'fresh' blood. A haemorrhage into the right pleural (chest) cavity from a lung injury still appeared as dark red fluid (although the microscopic cellular structure had changed). Heart and intestines were intact, and when the liver was cut open, its surface was bright pink, although this faded quickly to brown. Such a degree of preservation had clearly depended on rapid embalming and the body's enclosure within lead, clay packing and wooden coffin. There was also evidence of adipocere development, whereby fatty acids are deposited *post mortem* within the tissues, leading to their dehydration and acidification with a consequent deterrence of microbial activity which would otherwise cause putrefaction.

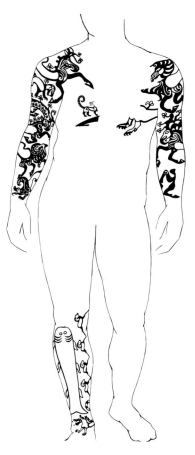

Frozen Scythians

The Scythians, tribal groups living on the steppes to the north and north-east of the Black Sea, developed into dynamic, artistic, pastoral peoples between the seventh and third centuries BC. A series of barrows in the High Altai region of southern Siberia has yielded some unusually well-preserved objects, including human remains. The special conditions inside these tombs are the result of permafrost forming deep within them, and excavations between the 1920s and 1950s at the sites of Shibe, Pazyryk, Bashadar and Tuekta produced a remarkable collection of organic material. Human remains, fur, textiles and wood were all preserved, sometimes even with their original colours.

The discovery of body tattoos confirmed the remark by the Greek historian Herodotus, in the fifth century BC, that brave and renowned warriors were thus decorated. One such chieftain, from barrow 2 at Pazyryk, shows good preservation of the skin, with elaborate tattoos extending from the arms onto the chest and on the lower leg (Plate IV). These were produced by pricking deep into the skin and introducing dark colouring substances into the minute holes.

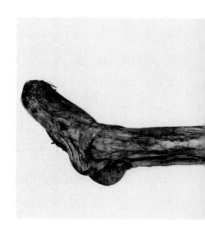

Early Egyptian kings are not alone in having suffered at the hands of tomb-robbers, and the head of one Pazyryk chieftain had been hacked off and removed from the coffin. As a result, it is less well preserved than the rest of the body. Like the Egyptians also, the Scythians achieved a high level of embalming. In one body from Pazyryk this involved long incisions, all of which were skilfully stitched up.

81 Diagram of the tattoos on the body of the Scythian chieftain from barrow 2 at Pazyryk. The highly conventionalised but very expressive animal designs include a wild ass and mountain ram as well as 'fantastic' creations of a winged animal with a feline tail and a deer with a bird's beak.

Canary Islands

In the *Monthly Chronicle* for January 1773 it was recorded that Captain Young, commander of a sloop called the *Weasel*, called in at Tenerife in the Canary Islands on a return journey from Guinea. While exploring the island he came upon a cave in which he found several ancient bodies which, according to the *Chronicle*, were 'sewed up in goat skins'. Some of the bodies, it was recorded, were 'seven feet long', and others only a little over five feet. On opening up one of the skins, Captain Young found a well-preserved corpse. He then 'expressed a great desire to obtain one of these bodies; but the Romish Priest made many objections. Those, however, a little gold removed, and he procured him a female Mummy.' The body was brought to Britain and given to Trinity College, Cambridge. The authorities eventually passed it on to the Faculty of Archaeology and Anthropology, where it was found to be a male with the penis removed. However, in view of its other physical attributes, it seems very unlikely that Captain Young was deceived as to the sex of this ancient Guanche.

Literary evidence suggests that by the time of the Spanish conquest of these islands in 1402, the indigenous Guanche people had long been using some of the volcanic caves as burial chambers. Sadly, of the hundreds of bodies thought to have been found at that time, very few are still available for study. The Cambridge body is thus important. Although we are no longer able to make comparisons with other Guanche mummies, this one at least was extremely well preserved, with a brown, leathery skin. It had been embalmed in a similar fashion to Egyptian mummies, and had a large abdominal incision (neatly stitched up) through which the intestines had been removed and vegetable packing inserted into the abdomen and thighs.

82 Full-length view of the Guanche mummy now in Cambridge.

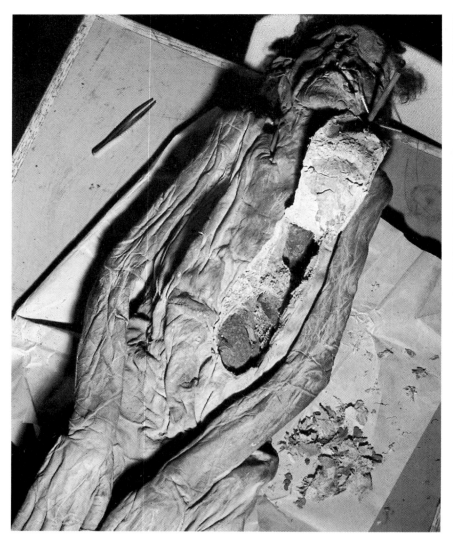

83 Tissue-sampling the Cambridge Guanche mummy. Part of the trunk is flapped open so that dried lung and abdominal packing can be seen.

Generally speaking, the treatment of the body was reminiscent of that of an Egyptian mummy of the Twenty-first Dynasty. However, in contrast to the usually more fragile soft tissue of Egyptian bodies, the Guanche body is remarkably tough and in far better condition.

As the thorax was not 'cleaned out', the heart and the shrunken but intact lungs were still present. In puzzling contrast, the brain seems to have decayed, possibly as a result of serious damage to the head and face at, or just after, death. In fact, other tissues also showed microscopic evidence of some degree of decay and in particular the presence of fungal hyphae.

84 A late predynastic body from Gebelein, Egypt, originally placed in a wicker basket and covered in mammal skin. The individual appears to be elderly and shows bone loss, probably due to senile osteoporosis (British Museum).

Egypt

While the Canary Islands have a mild climate and the caves are an especially protected micro-environment, the arid conditions along much of the Nile valley and extending into Nubia have encouraged natural desiccation, and dried bodies have been found dating from as far back as the predynastic period, 5,000 years ago. Special treatment of the body – mummification, with linen wrappings impregnated with resin – had developed by early dynastic times. The Egyptian embalmers were quick to understand the process of decomposition, and their job was to try to assist the natural preservation of soft tissue. Evisceration (removal of the intestinal tract) therefore became common, as did the extraction of the brain through the nose. Moreover, the embalmers were aware that drying out and shrinkage could occur, and at times tried to counteract this and maintain the original shape of the body by modelling and inserting shapes into the wrappings. Thus in the necropolis of Giza, a woman in shaft B of tomb 2220 had false breasts modelled from linen, and a body from tomb 17 at Meydum had a penis modelled in cloth.

85 The amputated right leg of the Egyptian mummy 1770, with internal 'splints' for attachment to an artificial limb.

86 Packing in the trunk of mummy 1770, inserted following evisceration.

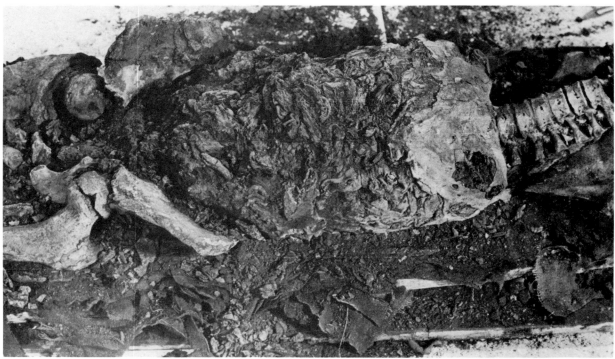

87 The toes of the Cambridge Guanche mummy, showing the thongs which were used to hold the nails in place. The toe- and fingernails of Egyptian mummies were also tied on during mummification.

Interest in, and standards of, mummification varied through time, and, for the commoner, natural desiccation was the only chance of survival. In an Eleventh Dynasty group of female bodies from Deir el-Bahri, drying out and preservation had been aided by the application of dry natron and resin to the outer surface. Some of these 'princesses' are tattooed, a rarity which also occurs in Greenlandic, Scythian and a few Peruvian bodies. By the New Kingdom (1470–1070 BC), even higher standards of embalming had been attained, for social dignitaries at least. Internal organs were washed, soaked in natron, further treated with hot resin, wrapped, and then packed in 'canopic jars'. As in the case of the Cambridge Guanche mummy, toe- and fingernails were tied on to ensure that they did not fall off during this period of treatment, especially during the application of dry natron. Elaborate packing of the body cavities then proceeded, followed by skin-surface applications, especially of resin, and elaborate bandaging. Relevant incantations accompanied each stage. By the seventieth day, the trussed-up corpse was ready for its coffin.

Looking at the unwrapped Egyptian mummies or naturally dried bodies in the displays in the British Museum or elsewhere, one's first impression is that these ancient people are still wonderfully lifelike, and indeed it is remarkable that they have preserved so well over six thousand years. However, in comparison with some other archaeological bodies, including those from European bogs, they have a dry fragility which suggests that an arid environment is not necessarily the best for preserving human soft tissue.

Greenland

A number of bodies of medieval date have been found in Greenland, preserved by a natural freeze-drying process. In some instances these have been even better preserved than the ancient frozen Scythian bodies. Following the initial discovery of some remains in 1972, two graves at the ancient settlement of Qilakitsoq on Greenland's west coast yielded eight bodies. Some time around AD 1450, the bodies had been placed under a rock overhang and, instead of putrefying, had gradually freeze-dried in this 'niche' protected from sun, snow and rain. Their clothing, beautifully made from skins of reindeer, seals, goose, cormorant, eider duck, mallard and red-throated diver, was similarly in very fine condition.

The graves contained six women, a baby (Plate VII) and a boy with a serious hip condition known as Calve-Perthe's disease. One of the women had cancer of the throat (a naso-pharyngeal tumour), which has a puzzlingly high frequency in modern Greenlandic Eskimos. Changes had probably occurred in the bodies shortly after death, but the process of decay had soon been stopped by the natural freeze-drying. Fine tattoo lines were found on the faces of all but the youngest of the women. These were no longer visible by normal light, but were revealed by infra-red photography. The tattoos are thought in this case to have been made by easing a needle and soot-covered thread through the outer layers of the skin.

88 The warm and wind-proof anorak worn by one of the Eskimos from Qilakitsok, Greenland (Greenland Museum).

The term 'freeze-drying' as used here does not imply exactly the same process as the laboratory treatment of Lindow Man. The micro-environment of the Greenlandic grave encouraged drying out after the bodies had become very cold. Thus, in contrast to laboratory freeze-drying, the ancient Eskimo tissue showed considerable shrinkage and marked discolouration. It might have been possible to restore the original body 'plumpness' by rehydration (a technique tried out with success on one of the hands of the Cambridge Guanche mummy). However, there is at present no satisfactory method of restoring original flesh colour (except of course by unacceptable means such as bleaching and staining the tissues).

China

The chance nature of so much archaeological discovery is well illustrated by the finding of human remains in China. Two decades ago, although many skeletons of early Chinese peoples had been ex-cavated, their condition would not have suggested that one could look forward to the eventual discovery of extremely well-preserved bodies. Yet this has happened, and one is left wondering whether more exciting discoveries of this kind are still to follow. Two dynastic periods are so far involved, the Han dynasty (206 BC–AD 220) and the Sung dynasty (AD 960–1279). The bodies were therefore roughly contemporary with the European bog bodies, the St Bees knight and some of the ancient Amerindians of Arizona.

The earliest of these exciting tombs is in the suburbs of the city of Changsha, Hunan province, and dates from the Western Han dynasty (206 BC–AD 24). During industrial development in 1972, a rectangular

89 Diagrammatic section through the deep pit tomb which contained the large Han period coffin of Lady Dai (after Rudolph).

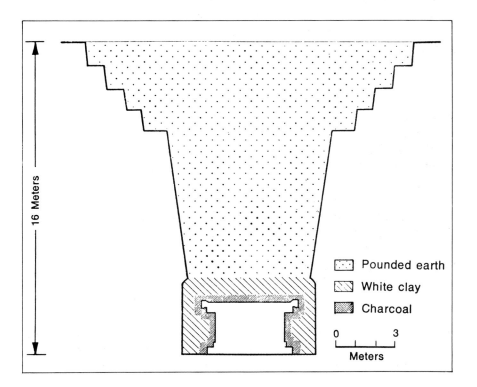

16 Meters

Pounded earth
White clay
Charcoal

0   3
Meters

shaft 16 metres deep was found under a tomb mound. At the bottom
was a sturdy timber structure, into which were sleeved six success-
ively larger coffins. This was covered by many layers of bamboo
matting followed by a layer of charcoal around which was white clay,
and finally the deep shaft was filled with pounded earth. Surrounding
the innermost coffin were five others which had over 1,000 objects in
them. The inner coffin contained the extremely well-preserved body
now identified as Lady Dai, a woman of about 50 years of age. Some
twenty layers of silk fabrics surrounded her, and also within the tomb
were pottery, food offerings, wooden articles and lacquer-ware.

Although the elaborate food offerings of rice and rice cakes,
melons, pears, peaches, pickled vegetables, fish, eggs and chickens,
deer, beef, pig, dog and rabbit show that Lady Dai was used to plenty
of variety and nourishment, nevertheless she seems to have suffered
from tuberculosis (shown by calcified areas of the lungs). She was
only about five feet in height, and was relatively plump. Indeed, over-
eating may have encouraged the development of her circulation
problems (atherosclerosis) as well, perhaps, as her serious gallstones.
Her death may have been caused by a heart attack following acute
gall-bladder pain. Judging by the 138 melon seeds in her stomach and
intestines, she had been eating melon just before death overtook her.
Histological and microscopic studies showed that the body was in a
remarkably good state of preservation, with intact internal organs,
and blood vessels, muscles and nerves could even be identified. Some
bacterial spores were also seen in the tissues. One can only guess that
this remarkable preservation was due to rapid burial into the cool and
anaerobic environment of this deep shaft grave, sealed off in charcoal
and clay.

In July 1975 the tomb of Chou Yü in Chin-t'an county yielded
another remarkable body. It was a typical southern Sung tomb in
structure and furniture, and contained a considerable quantity of

90 The well-preserved Han
dynasty body of Lady Dai
(Changsha, Hunan Prov-
incial Museum).

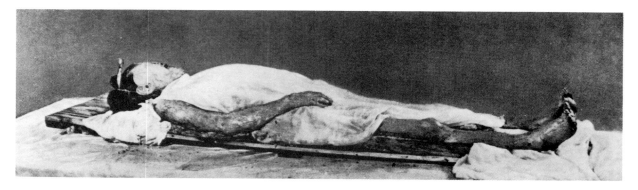

91 The body from the Sung tomb of Chou Yü, with Chinese scientists demonstrating the flexibility of the corpse (Jiangsu Province, Jintan Museum).

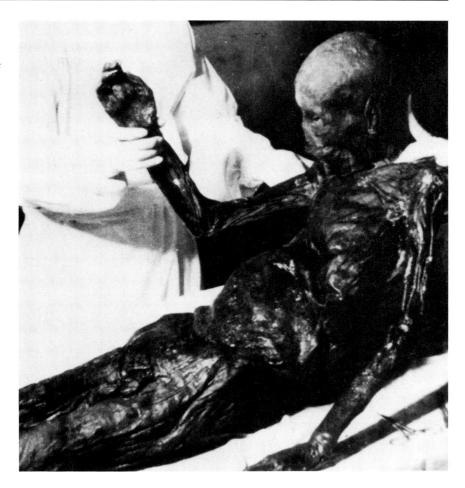

well-preserved, colourful silk garments and beautifully designed fabrics. It also produced a rare hand-written copy of a certificate of a student of the Imperial College. The body was that of a male, and like Lady Dai it had remained remarkably soft and supple, and it was possible to undertake detailed studies of the tissues. Like Lindow Man, he had suffered from the intestinal worms *Trichuris* and *Ascaris*.

Japan

Japan has yet to produce any extremely ancient well-preserved bodies but there are some more recent examples, dated for the most part between about 1360 and 1900. Although the temperate and relatively humid climate may not seem conducive to the survival of bodies, aspects of Japanese Buddhism have encouraged the 'mummification' of human remains. Of the various bodies remaining today, most are those of priests who undertook 'self-mummification' by ascetism and gradual starvation. The oldest body, that of the priest Kochi, dates from 1363 and is preserved in Saisho-ji Temple, Teradomari City. There are signs that some deterioration has taken place in this individual during the past century, with areas of damage made by rats.

Treatment of priests after death was variable. Tetsumonkai (died 1829) was dried out by candles, while Tetsuryūkai was buried, then exhumed and embalmed. These few bodies have been studied in detail by Japanese scientists. Although the number is statistically small, it is nevertheless interesting to see that the A gene frequency of the ABO blood-group system is much higher in these bodies than in modern data on the Japanese. An earlier study of four Japanese governor-generals of the twelfth century AD showed an equal occurrence of gene A and gene B, so there is a puzzling deficiency of gene O in the sample as a whole.

Oceania

Moving to New Guinea, Australia and the Pacific, we find few preserved bodies, but a surprising amount of information about practices for preserving the dead. In Australia particularly, bodies have been preserved by chance in arid localities, but drying and smoking techniques seem to have been widely practised. While in most of the world special methods of preservation other than modern mortuary practices are extinct, it is recorded that as recently as 1963 the preserved body of a tribal leader from Laiagam was brought to the Mount Hagen Agricultural Show, because before his death he had expressed a wish to attend it! However, more usual reasons for attempting to preserve people were feelings of loss and grief, a desire to protect the dead from spirits, or, in the case of special individuals, the requirement to follow an established formality. Most actual evidence of these practices, in the form of mummies, has come from around the Torres Strait between Australia and New Guinea.

Figs 92 and 93 show a typical 'mummy' of this kind. In its final resting state, it is indeed a fragile husk of its former self. The methods which were used to produce such a mummy are fairly well documented. A few days after death, the body was taken out to sea, and there stripped of its outer skin (epidermis). The intestinal tract was removed and the cavity stuffed with palm pith, and finally the brain was extracted. Back on shore, the body was mounted on a wooden framework and hung to dry. Later, artificial eyes were fixed in position and red ochre applied to the body.

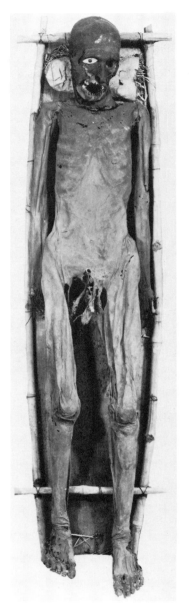

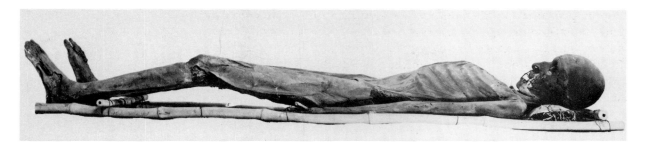

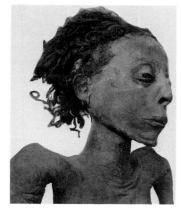

92 (*left*) and 93 (*top*) Front and side views of a Torres Strait 'mummy' (British Museum, Natural History).

94 (*above*) Head and shoulders of the Egyptian princess Nes-ta-neb-ashru, showing large artificial eyes (Cairo Museum). Compare with Fig. 95.

95 The head of the Torres Strait body, showing an artificial eye still in position.

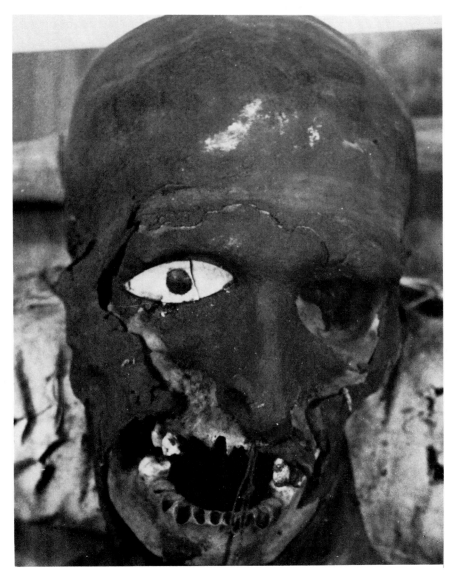

The New World

The nature of archaeological human remains differs widely throughout the Americas, and it will therefore be convenient to consider three important areas separately. They differ not only in cultural terms but also from the point of view of the types of local environment which have allowed the soft tissue to survive. We shall not be concerned here with somewhat exotic human specimens, such as Jivaro shrunken heads, which do not have archaeological relevance.

The far north-west (Alaska and Aleutian Islands)

The climate in this area is by no means homogeneous, Alaska being colder and the Aleutians somewhat damper. As with the Scythians of Siberia, the Alaskan permafrost has encouraged excellent preservation, again to the extent that tattoo marks on the arms of one body could be clearly studied. This was an Eskimo woman found on Saint Lawrence Island, dated to about AD 300–500 and reported on by Michael Zimmerman and George Smith. She had apparently been accidentally asphyxiated (with bronchial haemorrhage and some breathed-in moss fibres). Other evidence of pathology included coronary artery disease and a hair-line skull fracture, and in the faeces were ova of a fish worm (*Cryptocotyle lingua*). Like the Cambridge Guanche body and some Egyptian mummies, she had anthracosis from the long-term inhalation of cooking-fire smoke.

96 Female Aleut mummy (Washington, Smithsonian Institution).

In the Aleutian Islands, on the other hand, although the climate is cold and damp, the dead were kept in volcanically warmed caves which were remarkably dry. A large number of Aleutian bodies were found about fifty years ago and transported to the Smithsonian Institution in Washington. Some of these had undergone evisceration; no doubt this special treatment was reserved for people of importance. Dry grass was used to stuff the cavity. The body was usually bound and in a flexed position, like Peruvian mummy bundles. Natural drying processes are thought to have been enhanced by periodic intentional drying of the outer surface, by wiping and even by suspension above a fire.

In the case of an Aleut 'commoner' from one of these caves, examined by Dr Zimmerman and his colleagues, there was clear evidence that he died of lobar pneumonia. Once again, other pathology included anthracosis of the lungs, no doubt from breathing in fire smoke.

Although the few individuals of these sub-Arctic cultures so far studied in detail have yielded a great deal of information about parasites, inflammation and even arterial disease, we still know relatively little about them, considering the number of bodies which have been preserved. Much work still remains to be done in this area, preferably using non-destructive techniques as far as possible.

The rest of North America
This second 'zone' of the Americas has produced preserved bodies from somewhat divergent areas ecologically, generally dated to between 100 BC and AD 1400. South of the Great Lakes, in the Kentucky region, lived eastern woodland hunter-gatherers and farmers. In the south-west were desert gatherers and cultivators adapted to the challenges of more arid environments. Perhaps surprisingly, both areas have produced bodies of ancient Amerindians.

The first 'mummies' from the Mammoth Cave area of Kentucky were found by saltpetre miners as early as 1811. The body called 'Fawn Hoof' appeared in 1813, but is now only preserved as a skeleton. In 1835 came 'Lost John', an Amerindian killed in a mining accident. He sustained fractures to various parts of his body, and died probably as a result of a crushed chest. In 1875, Salts Cave yielded the body of a slender boy, first called 'Little Alice', then 'Al' when closer inspection revealed external genitals. A radiocarbon date suggests that he died in the first century BC. Various other mummies have been found in this general area of Mammoth Cave National Park and extending into Tennessee, but have not received the detailed attention of those mentioned here.

It is said that the Navajos who live in the south-west, in the region of the Canyon de Chelly and Canyon del Muerto, call the local caves 'haunted houses'. On looking at the well-preserved bodies from these caves and the surrounding area, one can understand their reluctance to disturb the ancient dead. The earliest of these 'mummies', which are in fact naturally preserved remains, are those of semi-nomadic hunter-gatherers known as Basketmakers (AD 100–700). They may be flexed or unflexed and are usually wrapped in fur blankets or tanned skins, although children may be treated slightly differently. Most are from caves and rock shelters, and various objects may be buried with them, including weapons, pipes, ornaments and baskets. From Arizona, in particular, come parts of at least forty bodies, some of which have been studied. Especially well-preserved bodies were found there in Ventana Cave (AD 1000–1400) and Vandal Cave (AD 500–1250). As yet, however, surprisingly few detailed investigations have been undertaken on this group of ancient Amerindians.

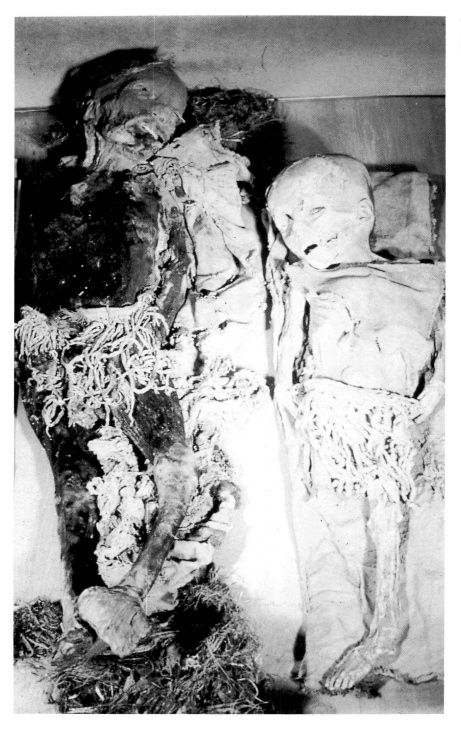

97 Dried bodies of ancient Amerindian children (Arizona, Montezuma Castle).

98 Peruvian mummy being carried on a stretcher during a 'festival of the dead' in November.

South America

The early peoples of the Andean area of South America evolved some of the most complex societies of late prehistory, in particular the Inca empire, which eventually extended from Ecuador in the north to Chile and Bolivia in the south. The arid coastlands and the much colder, dry atmosphere of the higher Andes have both encouraged the preservation of human bodies (Plate VI). Perhaps the majority of dried human remains were naturally desiccated, but intentional preservation of Inca kings and dignitaries was also widely practised. Indeed, soon after European contact with the New World, these preserved representatives of the ancient past became a source of wonder to the intrusive Hispanic society of the sixteenth century. The remains of three Inca kings and two 'queens' were sent to Lima in 1560 and twenty years later were still in fine condition. The indigenous Inca peoples venerated their noble ancestors and during the November 'festival of the dead' the mummies would be brought out and paraded on stretchers.

Writing in the Inca capital, Cuzco, in 1559, Polo de Ondegardo says: 'The bodies were so intact that they lacked neither hair, eyebrows nor eyelashes. They were in clothes just as they had worn when alive, with *llautus* [bands] on their heads but no other sign of royalty. They were seated in the way Indian men and women usually sit, and their eyes were cast down . . . The bodies weighed so little that any Indian could carry them from house to house in his arms or on his shoulders.'

While some of these bodies appear to have been embalmed with applications of a 'balsam' or 'bitumen' and possibly herbs, good descriptions of such techniques are regrettably not available. In fact, it seems unlikely that many were given this kind of special treatment, which may have included smoke curing. It also seems unlikely that many of the Peruvian remains we now have for study underwent evisceration or had any packing inserted under the skin. It is common, however, to find the bodies well wrapped, the nature of the covers depending on the period and the importance of the individual. Bird skins, mammal hides, textiles of varying quality, and reed matting and grass cord were all used. Many of the remains are in the form of tightly flexed 'mummy bundles', and X-rays of these sometimes reveal necklaces, bracelets and other ornaments or special objects wrapped with the dead.

Most of the better-preserved bodies are from the arid coastal zone, but the cold higher altitudes have produced some surprises. For instance, in 1954 the naturally freeze-dried body of an 8- to 10-year-

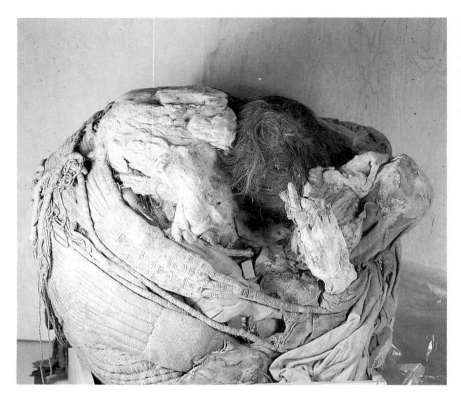

99 Peruvian mummy bundle. Except for the head and hands, the body is tightly wrapped in fine-quality fabrics (University of California, Berkeley, Museum of Anthropology).

old boy, dressed in a camelid wool poncho, was found in an Inca-period tomb at Cerra El Plomo. Whether, as some have suggested, he was a 'sacrifice' of some kind and had been left there to die, is debatable, for he could equally have died as a result of an undetected infectious disease.

Only a limited amount of research into the health of these early South Americans has yet been accomplished (some of the findings have been discussed in the section on disease). The two most important discoveries so far relate to tuberculosis and hookworm disease. There has long been a debate as to whether tuberculosis was present in the indigenous peoples of South America before the arrival of Europeans. Although previous finds had suggested that it was, the problem was resolved in 1973 by the discovery of an 8-year-old Peruvian child of the Nasca period (AD 200–800). Drs Allison and Pezzia found marked spinal tuberculosis in the body, with not only bone involvement but also a typical associated abscess in the psoas hip-muscles, tracking down from the spinal inflammation. Moreover, tubercular nodules were seen on the lung, pleura and part of the kidney. Stained preparations from these infected soft tissues re-

100 Very well-preserved Colombian mummy from a cave in the Bogota region. Discovered in 1842 with 27 others, little remains of them today (Museum of Mankind).

vealed clumps of acid-fast bacilli, quite possibly of tubercular origin.

The American origins of hookworm infection, caused by *Ancylostoma duodenale*, an unpleasant intestinal worm which can cause much bleeding and often serious anaemia, have also been debated. Some scientists thought the worm had arrived with the Negro slaves from Africa, but an ancient Peruvian body from the Tiahuanaco period, dated to about AD 920 ± 30 years, has now proved otherwise. By great good fortune, the intestine was sufficiently well preserved to enable it to be opened up and viewed under the microscope. For the medical biologists involved, it must have been rather like peering at the treasures of Tutankhamun for the first time, for there, on the inner surface of the gut, they saw worms still clearly attached. Under the scanning electron microscope, the morphology of the 'teeth' and other characteristic aspects of the head region showed up distinctly, leaving no doubt that this was indeed the destructive hookworm.

Conclusion

Ah me, sweet Death, you are the only god
Who comes as a servant when he is called, you know,
Listen then to this sound I make, it is sharp,
Come, Death. Do not be slow.

Stevie Smith

The discovery of Lindow Man has provided an opportunity for reviewing what has been done and, ideally, what should be done when well-preserved human remains are found. Lindow Man himself has probably had more specialist attention and more specialist equipment brought to his investigation than any previous individual. Having said that, it is clear from our review of other recent studies that high levels of enquiry are being achieved on material from Egypt, China and elsewhere.

We have seen that a variety of environments – bogs, deserts, permafrost, even deep and well-sealed tombs in more temperate climates – may all yield instances of remarkable preservation. By investigating them, we are slowly piecing together evidence of ancient causes of death and rituals associated with it. We can begin to answer questions about the social status and backgrounds of the individuals studied and about the attitude towards death in the culture to which they belonged. From the evidence of pollen, larger plant debris, insects or other species found in the earth surrounding the body, we can build up some impression of the environment in which these individuals lived. Similar microscopic investigations of their gut contents provide us with information about foods eaten, including perhaps the ritual intake of plants such as mistletoe or ergot, and may even sometimes give clues to the season of death.

Detailed study of the bodies themselves may tell us about physique, 'embalming' methods, health or disease, sex and age. Knowledge of the biochemistry of bodies is slowly expanding, and early studies on blood groups and blood stains are extending into a consideration of trace element composition and even the possibility of DNA cloning. In some of these studies, optimism must be tempered with considerable scientific caution.

Lindow Man truly looks 'at rest' now, and perhaps there is a message for us all in this figure who suffered such violence. Death has wiped away all the struggle, all the pain, all the anguish and fear, and even all his past joys. In our 'advanced' society, where matters of death and violence are all too commonplace, we nevertheless hasten it out of the way, disposing of it through well-established funerary practices. In the bodies from the past, we are reminded of its certainty, then as now. In a way, even at the moment when they yield up something of their lives, there is a quiet dignity about these ancient dead. One feels intuitively that there is no harm in examining them and discovering something of their past. Scientific enquiry is not prying for the sake of it: only the truth is being sought. While, therefore, one can understand those who have found ancient human remains and superstitiously or religiously covered them over again, it seems to me that our ancestors, even those of only a few generations ago, are nevertheless an integral part of our archaeology and history. If we are to enquire into history at all, if the past is truly a useful perspective for the present and future, then we have the dual commitment of honouring the dead and studying and describing them.

We must humbly respect the attitudes and rituals of the past, but the dead cannot control the present and the future. The crypt of a church may be needed more desperately for the homeless living than as an ossuary. City development may uproot ancient burials, which cannot stand in the way of change. Where disturbance is inevitable, the investigation of excavated bones or bodies and their scientific evaluation simply establishes their importance prior to reburial or conservation in some alternative situation. It is understandable that some Amerindian communities in the New World and the aborigines of Australia wish to take back their 'own kind', even to the extent of removing ancient remains from museums if they are seen as part of their ancestry. The ethics of such activities are complex, and political solutions usually all too hasty. Does each religious sect, each culturally distinguishable component of humanity at large, have the right to claim, withdraw, keep to itself those remains which it sees as its ancestors and its responsibility? Will the tug-of-war antics surrounding the remains claimed to be those of St Edward the Martyr become commonplace? What in fact are our rights in relation to the people of the past? While the philosophy of biology teaches us about variation, it seems to me that it also emphasises the essential brotherhood of everyone alive today, and the need for compassion and feelings of affinity beyond culture and territory. The inhumanity of high finance and the absurd national distortions of politics and religion make fools of us all. Poverty stares at lands of plenty, and death comes as a friend to the starved and diseased. So many die violently, though most of us long for peace and tranquillity.

Archaeology contributes to this history of human folly, of courage and of waste. In this vast story, the ancient dead also have their part to play. As yet they have been little investigated, but they deserve more consideration. At least, that is what the investigations on Lindow Man would seem to indicate.

It may well be that Shakespeare was right in the famous philosophical comments on the human condition he put into the mouth of Macbeth; but archaeology, including the study of actual human remains, at least provides one more chance for figures from the past to appear again 'on stage':

> Tomorrow, and tomorrow, and tomorrow,
> Creeps in this petty pace from day to day,
> To the last syllable of recorded time;
> And all our yesterdays have lighted fools
> The way to dusty death. Out, out, brief candle!
> Life's but a walking shadow, a poor player,
> That struts and frets his hour upon the stage,
> And then is heard no more.
>
> Macbeth, *V, scene V*

Bibliography

Some Further Reading

Andersen, S. R., and Geertinger, P. 1984. Bog bodies investigated in the light of forensic medicine. *Journal of Danish Archaeology* 3: 111–19.

Andrews, Carol. 1984. *Egyptian Mummies*. London: British Museum Publications.

Brothwell, D. R., Sandison, A. T., and Gray, P. H. K. 1969. Human biological observations on a guanche mummy with anthracosis. *American Journal of Physical Anthropology* 30: 333–47.

Cockburn, A., and Cockburn, E. (eds). 1980. *Mummies, Disease and Ancient Cultures*. Cambridge: University Press. (This book contains a series of review papers on bodies from different parts of the world.)

David, Rosalie, and Tapp, E. (eds). 1984. *Evidence Embalmed. Modern Medicine and the Mummies of Ancient Egypt*. Manchester: University Press.

Glob, P. V. 1969. *The Bog People. Iron-Age Man Preserved*. London: Faber and Faber.

Hansen, J. P. H., Meldgaard, J., and Nordqvist, J. 1985. The mummies of Qilakitsoq. *National Geographic* 167: 190–207.

Helbaek, H. 1958. The last meal of Grauballe Man. *Kuml*: 83–116. (See also *Kuml* 1956: 99–163, for other studies of the Grauballe individual.)

Munksgaard, E. 1984. Bog bodies – a brief survey of interpretations. *Journal of Danish Archaeology* 3: 120–23.

Rudenko, S. I. 1970. *Frozen Tombs of Siberia. The Pazyryk Burials of Iron Age Horsemen*. London: Dent.

Rudolph, R. C. 1973. Two recently discovered Han tombs. *Archaeology* 26: 106–15.

Stead, I. M., Bourke, J. B., and Brothwell, Don (eds). 1986. *Lindow Man. The Body in the Bog*. London: British Museum Publications. (This consists of the collected specialist papers on Lindow Man.)

Other References

Allison, M. J., and Pezzia, A. 1973–74. Preparation of the dead in pre-Columbian coastal Peru. *Paleopathology Newsletter* 4: 10–12; 5: 7–9.

Boyd, W. C., and Boyd, L. G. 1934. An attempt to determine the blood group of mummies. *Proceedings of the Society of Experimental Biology and Medicine* 31: 67.

Boyd, W. C., and Boyd, L. G. 1937. Blood grouping tests on 300 mummies. *Journal of Immunology* 32: 307–9.

Candela, P. B. 1939. Blood group determinations upon the bones of thirty Aleutian mummies. *American Journal of physical Anthropology* 24: 361–83.

Connolly, R. C., and Harrison, R. D. 1969. Kinship of Smenkhkare and Tutankhamen affirmed by serological micro method. *Nature* CCIV: 325.

David, R. (ed.) 1978. *Mysteries of the Mummies. The Story of the Manchester University Investigation*. London: Book Club Associates.

Elliot Smith, G., and Dawson, W. R. 1924. *Egyptian Mummies*. London: Allen and Unwin.

Gebühr, M. 1979. Das Kindergrab von Windeby. Versuch einer 'Rehabilitation'. *Offa* 36: 75–107.

Green, C. S., Paterson, M., and Biek, L. 1981. A Roman coffin-burial from the Crown Buildings site, Dorchester: with particular reference to the head of well-preserved hair. *Proceedings of the Dorset Natural History and Archaeological Society* 103: 67–100.

Guozhang, Z., Wenhui, F., Yiheng, B., Jinian, X., and Yunshu, Y. 1979. Microscopic and submicroscopic studies on the peripheral nerve and skeletal muscle of the female cadaver found in the Han tomb No. 1. *Scientia Sinica* 22: 1095–8.

Haury, E. W. 1975. *The Stratigraphy and Archaeology of Ventana Cave*. Tucson: University of Arizona Press.

Jørgensen, S. 1956. The finding-place of Grauballe Man. *Kuml*: 114-30.

Landweer, G. J. 1904. Twee Oud-Germaansche lijken uit het Werdingerveen. *Eigen Haard* 30: 597–600.

Liversage, D. 1984. La femme de Huldremose. In *Eléments de Pré- et Protohistoire Européenne. Hommages à Jacques-Pierre Millotte*. Paris: Belles Lettres.

Loy, T. H. 1985. Recent advances in blood residue analysis. *Proceedings of the Second Australian Archaeometry Conference*. In press.

Munck, W. 1956. Pathological-anatomical and forensic-medicinal investigation of the peat-bog body from Grauballe. *Kuml*: 131–7.

Munizaga, J., Allison, M. J., and Aspillaga, E. 1978. Diaphragmatic hernia associated with strangulation of the small bowel in an Atacamena mummy. *American Journal of Physical Anthropology* 48: 17–20.

Munizaga, J., Allison, M. J., and Paredas, C. 1978. Cholelithiasis and cholecystitis in pre-Columbian Chileans. *American Journal of Physical Anthropology* 48: 209–12.

Murphy, R. 1972. Medieval textiles, Tawnamore td., Co. Sligo. *Journal of the Royal Society of Antiquaries of Ireland* 102: 215–22.

Pahl, W. M. 1980. Computed tomography – a new radiodiagnostical technique applied to medico-archaeological investigation of Egyptian mummies. *Ossa* 7: 189–98.

Rabino-Massa, E., and Chiarelli, B. 1972. The histology of naturally desiccated and mummified bodies. *Journal of Human Evolution* 1: 259–62.

Robbins, L. M. 1974. Prehistoric people of the Mammoth Cave area. In Watson, P. J. (ed.), *Archeology of the Mammoth Cave Area*, pp. 137–62. New York: Academic Press.

Sandison, A. T. 1963. The study of mummified and dried human tissue. In Brothwell, D. R., and Higgs, E. (eds), *Science in Archaeology*, pp. 490–502. London: Thames and Hudson.

Sandison, A. T. 1967. Diseases of the skin. In Brothwell, D. R., and Sandison, A. T. (eds), *Diseases in Antiquity*, pp. 449–56. Springfield: Thomas.

Tacitus, C., trans. Mattingly, H., rev. Handford, S.A. 1970. *Agricola* and *Germania*. Harmondsworth: Penguin.

Tapp, E., and O'Sullivan, D. 1982. St. Bee's Man: the autopsy. *Proceedings of the Paleopathology Association*, 4th European Meeting, pp. 178–82. Middelberg.

Zimmerman, M. R., Yeatman, G. W., and Sprinz, H. 1971. Examination of an Aleutian mummy. *Bulletin of the New York Academy of Medicine* 47: 80–103.

Zimmerman, M. R., and Smith, G. S. 1975. A probable case of accidental inhumation of 1600 years ago. *Bulletin of the New York Academy of Medicine* 51: 828–37.

Index

Numbers in bold type refer to illustrations